W9-AHP-372

THE SPRINGS OF LIBERTY

RETHINKING THEORY

GENERAL EDITOR

Gary Saul Morson

CONSULTING EDITORS

Robert Alter
Frederick Crews
John M. Ellis
Caryl Emerson

THE
SPRINGS OF
LIBERTY

The Satiric Tradition and Freedom of Speech

STEWART JUSTMAN

 NORTHWESTERN UNIVERSITY PRESS
EVANSTON, ILLINOIS

Northwestern University Press
Evanston, Illinois 60208-4210

Copyright © 1999 by Northwestern University Press.
Published 1999. All rights reserved.

Printed in the United States of America

ISBN 0-8101-1710-X

Library of Congress Cataloging-in-Publication Data

Justman, Stewart.
    The springs of liberty: the satiric tradition and freedom of
speech / Stewart Justman.
      p. cm.
    Includes bibliographical references and index.
    ISBN 0-8101-1710-X
    1. Satire, English—History and criticism.   2. Politics and
literature—Great Britain—History.   3. Political satire, English—
History and criticism.   4. Freedom of speech—Great Britain—
History.   5. Liberty in literature.   I. Title.
PR931.J87 1999
827.009'358—dc21   99–41486
                                                      CIP
The paper used in this publication meets the minimum requirements of the
American National Standard for Information Sciences—Permanence of Paper
for Printed Library Materials, ANSI Z39.48-1984.

Contents

Preface

In *The Psychological Mystique*, published in 1998 by Northwestern University Press, I asked how it is that psychology, concerned with the private regions of the self, could have become the lingua franca of a consumer society, its pretended insights our commonplaces and its jargon a public resource. In a similarly critical spirit, the present study tries to establish the precedence of the satiric tradition over both journalism—the very conduit of our clichés—and the terms of modern polemic. From satire, I suggest, flows the freedom of speech tied up in the repetitions of the press and the most familiar story lines of political argument. If law has codified a right of free speech, the spirit of free speech is to be found in the unformulaic spirit of satire.

Far from being bound to a narrow program of scorn and ridicule, the satiric tradition possesses both breadth and depth. One measure of what I call satire's excess—its power of overflowing any given scheme or genre—is the impossibility of reducing it to a single mode, message, or line of descent. In the pages that follow, accordingly, I trace two discordant satiric lines from Chaucer, each of them, however, a reminder of cultural wealth lost in a present divorced from the past.

Introduction

Myths, let us say, are stories a culture holds in common, originally stories of gods and heroes. In contrast to epic, however, the tales we call myth constitute less a literary genre than a sort of power prior to literature itself. Yet as ancient as myth is, it is still with us. The political creeds of the modern age are sometimes termed secular myths; no doubt it is power that they seek and find in myth in the first place.

I want to consider satire as a counterpart of myth. Satire strengthens groups in the sense that the primal satiric act of reviling some "other" has the effect of bonding the group behind it. If power comes into existence when people join together,[1] satire is indeed a well of power, seeing that nothing seems to unite us more effectually than common objects of ridicule and hatred, which satire supplies. Like myth, too, satire is arguably not a genre as such but a potential or fuel available to different genres, a source of literary power. The freedom of satire, which expresses itself in acts of license and excess—but also in literary innovation taking satire a long way from its presumptive origins—seems grounded in the fact that it can't be contained in or reduced to any given literary form. Again, satire like myth has been heavily exploited for nonliterary ends in the modern age. This study proposes that journalism and a great deal of political argument, whatever else may distinguish them, draw on a tradition of satire deeper and older than either. The power of satire is felt throughout literature. It has also been harnessed for a less cultural end: the mechanical reproduction of ideas.

*

With the rise of urban journalism in the nineteenth century went sensational stories of the dark side of city life.[2] By the end of the century the press, now stripping the veil from privacy as such, had worked out a formula for both meeting and piquing consumer demand that is still in use. Unauthorized photographs were published, the privacy of grief invaded. Divorce suits, gossip, proceedings of the criminal courts, anything, it seems, with a relish of scandal in it became daily fare. In the words of the *Yale Law Journal* in 1902, a sensational press had arrogated to itself "a right to pry into and grossly display before the public matters of the most private and personal concern."[3]

But while this sort of sensationalism made a display of bold novelty—brazen novelty to its critics—the act of spying into private life has roots in a

1

tradition far older than the tabloid press. In a satiric novel of 1707 an airborne devil removes the roofs from the houses of Madrid, allowing his companion to see into them "as plainly as . . . you see into a pie whose top is taken off."[4] And behind *Le Diable boiteux* in turn stands a history of satiric tales going back at least to that of Lucius, the ass who observes all, like the perfect spy. The device of *The Golden Ass* is but one available to a satiric tradition that claimed "the right to betray to the public a personal life, down to its most private and prurient little secrets,"[5] as in many of the *Canterbury Tales*, well before the practice was appropriated and standardized by the press. Indeed, not just the exploitation of scandal on the one hand and the decrying of abuses on the other, but freedom of speech itself took satiric form before being committed to the press and recognized by law.

Another device of exposure, the criminal trial, attains its supreme fictional realization alongside the metropolitan journalism of the late nineteenth century. I am thinking of the trial of Dmitri—an innocent man, as it happens; the actual murderer is nicknamed Balaam's ass—in *The Brothers Karamazov*. The trial of Dmitri is the focal point of public gossip within the work itself, the fascination of a world enraptured with the details of "the case"; and yet the press coverage and accompanying grandstanding, the dramatic scenes, the show character of the whole event seem to ensure only that the truth will be lost. In a distortion reminiscent of Swift, public and press seem to be staring at the affairs of the Karamazov family through a lens that both magnifies and inverts. It's as though the author's strong sense of the satiric tradition, and especially of Menippean satire, the "'journalistic' genre of antiquity,"[6] gave him a critical vantage on the world of journalism that he also knew from within. From a critical perspective of our own it appears that the novelty of invasive journalism lay not in the baring of private life as such but in the reduction of satiric license to a sales formula, along with a kind of stark literalism that insisted on the exposure of actual persons with photographic effect. Yet novelty may be a misnomer, inasmuch as the very standardization of the journalistic product—its provision on the daily schedule implied in the word "journalism" and enforced by the consumer economy—represents a negation of novelty. With his strong grounding in an ancient genre (and the immensity of his debt to tradition is brought out unforgettably by M. M. Bakhtin), Dostoevsky is capable of a novelty beyond the reach of a journalism that effaces the sense of the past only to reduce its "stories" to a form more generic than genre itself. Like the photographs and lithographs that by the turn of the century were being reproduced on a technological scale, the novelty of journalism issued in sheer repetition.[7]

This work is a study in memory, whose chief corrosive at present may be journalism. One effect of such corrosion is the lost cultural position of satire, whose privileges of ridicule and censure signally exemplify freedom of speech. Roman satire alone was "more outspoken than anything the Christian west could tolerate for nearly two thousand years";[8] now that taboos have fallen the memory of satire seems to have gone with them. The advent of civic journalism itself, however, corresponds with a form of satire adapted to a daily schedule and restrained within the limits of civility as if to demonstrate the rational use of liberty. If the penetration of private life was once a satiric device, journalism of a higher tone dates back to the periodical satires of Addison at the time of the formation of the modern public realm. Memory of the precursors of journalism as we know it has dimmed, though fragments of satire survive, as in the tactics of caricature so common in public debate. Yet satire, while employing caricature, cannot be reduced to it. The wealth of satire actually gives us something to weigh slogans and simplifications against, all the more because satire pioneers the freedom of speech now asserted by journalism and (as will be seen) originates propositions that have since become the currency of modern political argument. As in some family drama, satire has been upstaged by its own heir.

We are more likely to think of the novel as the kindred of journalism (having in mind, say, Defoe's double identity as novelist and journalist), and so it is. Growing up side by side, journalism and the modern novel are siblings, and the sort of aggressive disregard of the past shown in journalism today might be read as a reflection of the novel's show of disregarding traditional literary usage in favor of a more direct transcription of experience. The repudiation of tradition in the novel was far from complete, however. Incorporated into it as early as Cervantes was satire itself, a mode much older than journalism and disposed, as in Swift, to a critical view of the other's show of independence. In most of the works, including the novels, considered here, journalism accordingly becomes an *object* of satire as though in its focus on the moment it had lost its sense of the past. As in Dostoevsky where an opportunist makes a name for himself by writing articles about the Karamazov family—and opportunism defines many a journalist in the pages of fiction—journalism is subjected to the power of its own precursor.

The innovation of the modern novel rests largely on its circumstantiality —a new density of detail and description, a new concentration on the particulars of time, place, and person. Classically, such minutiae were outside the field of notice, on the theory that reality consists of "timeless universals" and the work of mimesis is to bring this changelessness into view. Behind the classical canon of the unity of time, for example, stands a conviction that since the course of time and details of change don't matter, "the truth about existence can be as fully unfolded in the space of a day as in the space of a lifetime."[9] Traces of this survive in *Ulysses*, which takes place over a day even as it demolishes classical decorum and offers details in an abundance—a satiric excess—beyond any conceivable formal requirement. From a classical perspective singular detail or physical specification tends to the grotesque, indeed the satiric, as with the fantastic details of Trimalchio's feast. We look in vain for the physical traits of Chaucer's Parson, but the Miller is specified down to the wart on his nose. And the tale the Miller tells (which like *Ulysses* plays off a classical antecedent) turns on twists of circumstance, not timeless universals; in fact, it treats the particulars of action with a kind of "journalistic" fidelity. The great fabliaux of the *Canterbury Tales*, prime among them the Miller's Tale, pose probably for the first time in literature the stark questions of who, what, when, where, why, how. Here all such logistical factors are attended to, converging in a trick where luck, timing, and location count as much as method. Reducing time and place, means and motive, to a kind of equality of the ridiculous, the Miller's Tale reminds us that the very elements of journalism were once the trappings of satire.

The fabliau, the lowest of literary forms, is in fact capable of high importance. When the underground of pre-Revolutionary Paris published their *libelles*—anecdotal accounts of the secret lives of the great, with their lechery on the one hand and impotence on the other—they converted the fabliau, in effect, into a lethal weapon of journalistic warfare. And it was out of the material of the *libelles* that the radical ideology of the French Revolution was forged.[10] Satire had hardened into a creed of sacred fury; had altogether lost the element of play. That element is restored in full in Byron's *Don Juan*, which makes a narrative technique of the spirit of improvisation that moves the tricksters of the fabliau (as when Nicholas in the Miller's Tale suddenly alters the jape). The element of play also returns in *Ulysses*, at its core the story of a wayward wife and cuckolded husband (with some lechery in him and some impotence)—generic figures worked up with such novelty that both transcend their definition, and with such richness that each seems flesh. As Joyce reclaims satire from the doctrinaire, so in its sheer excess of detail and allusion *Ulysses* seems to be getting back to the root meaning of satire, "full." Such plotting as there is in *Ulysses*, moreover, seems to follow roughly the same principle of the convergence of events informing the Miller's Tale.

Before launching into the ribaldry of the Miller's Tale, Chaucer offers a series of disclaimers evidently intended to win his audience's indulgence, the first and most notable alleging that he had no choice but to report the pilgrims' tales just as they were told. Pretending not to be the author but merely the recorder of the tales, and actually posing as this sorry figure, Chaucer requests and receives from his audience the license "not 'to be oneself'": a grant of satiric liberty that also, according to the conventions of satire, includes the right to expose private life.[11] If the invasion of privacy at the hands of the press obscures its own satiric original, so it seems the very act of report has a precedent in satire. In context, Chaucer's claim that he has to report the tales as they were severally delivered can mean only that of one like the Miller nothing but buffoonery can be expected (a twist on aesthetic decorum). And just as the exposure of private life was reduced to a routine of the metropolitan press, an artful pretense of fitting tale to teller was reduced to the plainness of a legal principle. According to a 1933 ruling in *People* v. *The Viking Press*, "The court may not require the author to put refined language into the mouths of primitive people."[12] (The Miller can't be expected to talk like the Knight.) The same doctrine figures in Judge Woolsey's decision of that year to admit *Ulysses* into the United States. In *Ulysses* itself the satiric license underlying freedom of speech—the license to overstep the bounds of propriety that was granted Chaucer and later formalized in law—attains one of its supreme expressions. Characteristically, the decline of the term "freedom of speech" to a formula, a dead letter, is in turn satirized in *Ulysses*. In the cliché-sodden style of "Eumaeus" Bloom is reported as "availing himself of the right of free speech" when he remarks on the beauty of the Italian language.[13]

Not just in the sense that satire precedes journalism into the world does satiric license underlie freedom of speech, of which journalism is now the institutional expression. Assuming all things could be accounted for by some single set of principles (and belief systems do make universal claims), maybe there would be no call for freedom of speech; certainly it would be pronounced an evil, a leader astray, a source of discord and confusion. Satire impresses on us that all things cannot be contained in a single viewpoint; that, as Northrop Frye puts it, "experience is bigger than any set of beliefs about it. The satirist demonstrates the infinite variety of what men do by showing the futility . . . of attempts to systematize or formulate a coherent scheme of what they do."[14] Fittingly, this resistance to definition applies as well to satire itself, which crosses from genre to genre and seems to defy critical efforts to pin down its nature,[15] the merit of Frye's theory of satire being precisely its breadth. At any event, not only does satire underwrite the reasoning of the Woolsey decision, it grounds freedom of speech altogether, showing up the pretense of dogmas and systems and making a virtue of what would otherwise be heresy.

The presumed author of the classic free-speech maxim, "I disapprove of what you say, but I will defend to the death your right to say it"—he has also been credited with founding investigative journalism—was a satirist of the keenest kind: Voltaire.[16]

Still more fundamentally, perhaps, satire underwrites freedom of speech in that beliefs take a freer, less hardened form in satire than in the political doctrines they have since become. The satiric principle that "attempts to systematize" are bound to fail, for example, is broader than the conservative doctrine it petrifies into, the doctrine that Nature defies our blueprints, being wiser than the human brain. It is so much broader that it also authorizes the contrary conviction (Byron's, for example) that all the conservative's efforts to lay down the law to human liberty are doomed to failure by Nature itself, like lashing the wind. In satire excess is of the essence, and the tradition as a whole possesses a kind of excess potential that in the modern age has been locked up by powerful doctrines; even the therapeutic creed that liberalism seems to have transformed itself into—even this presents a fractured reflection of the satiric project of curing delusion by showing us what we really are.[17] So, too, traditional exposés of vice, folly, and delusion give way to the ideological drive to bare the workings of the opponent's brain, a project no more enriching, arguably, than journalism's inside view of private life. In the case of Marxism, satire's probing of appearance and exposure of the fool and the knave become the "scientific" unmasking of opponents, an act of symbolic violence that progresses readily to something less symbolic (as was also the case in the most radical phase of the French Revolution). Coincidentally, the first political article Marx wrote is an attack, boiling with scorn and ridicule, on Prussian censorship. From its origin in satiric license Marxism itself would become a censorship machine beyond anything known to Prussia.

In America the press, which claims a professional interest in freedom of speech, now disseminates a kind of soft social science. Yet with its tendency "in general to treat 'higher' concepts in terms of 'lower' ones,"[18] social science itself has roots in satiric practices of debunking and reduction. Mandeville is a satirist on the verge of political economy, Bentham a philosophe who could still rail on occasion like a satirist, each offering a lowering analysis of human behavior. Satire per se is only too fond of reduction, of getting down to what the specimen really is, whether a miser, a cuckold, or just a fool. Yet for all its habit of reduction, satire at its best is distinguished by the quality of excess, an abundance that overflows the simplicity of formula and the boundaries of design.[19] We might call this quality freedom.

*

While the deceptions of memory in the consumer society don't come up to the Hitler-Stalin pact or the crimes of the managers of public memory in *Nineteen Eighty-four*, it seemed to one thoughtful postwar observer that even Americans "can often be persuaded by the mass media to hold an opinion opposite to the one held a few years ago, without remembering that it is the opposite."[20] The journalistic unit of time, however, isn't a year but a day. In the daily novelty of journalism violence against memory is both normalized and reduced, like the hostilities of a cold war. Unless journalism unwove itself every day it would not be news every day. As this implies, even the novelty of journalism is a novelty of the identical, a novelty that always seems to come to the same thing in the end.

And in consequence (and furtherance) of the erosion of memory in the consumer society, journalism loses touch with its sources in satire. Its more proximate link, as I have said, is with the very form that professes a neglect of preexisting models and makes a show of direct report, the novel. But if recognizably modern journalism, appearing on a regular schedule and commenting on events and trends, goes back to the formation of the public realm in the eighteenth century, this in turn took place amid a flowering of satire unparalleled in English letters either before or since. Satire seems as strongly linked with the category of the public as romance with the private. It's not only that Horace and Juvenal memorialize republican virtue and are honored in turn in the republic of letters in the eighteenth century. With its indictment of vice and folly, satire conveys something of the effect of trials that grip the public and somehow consummate its experience *as* a public, with a drama of accusation. The original satiric act would seem to be the public cursing of some evil one, a rite that declares and defines the common identity of all those who are parties to it.[21] The vitriol of satire survives in concentrations ranging from a primal ferocity to the most tempered irony to a kind of negated wrath in which the violence and excess of satire are themselves subjected to satire. Even as its tone was reduced and its prominence submerged by the more sentimental form of the novel, however, satire retained power to indict and convict. Even in the romance world of Dickens, with all of its improbability, satire maintains its keen critical edge as well as its old association with "the public square."

That Dickens, the master of caricature, and Twain, America's most celebrated satirist, also wrote journalism; that *Nineteen Eighty-four*, classed by the author as a satire, arises out of Orwell's journalistic writings—this affords a kind of presumption of a bond between journalism and satire. The bond itself is more than a matter of vocational overlap. It is grounded in the nature of satire itself. Though not confined to a single program or set of possibilities or even a single genre, satire tends to concentrate on the gap between profession and deed, theory and practice, the ideal and the actual—its way of exposing some denied truth serving as precedent, as it were, for the factuality of journalism.[22] There is an element of satire in the very notion of fact as something we run up against, something that confounds human pretensions. When Joyce writes, "In *Ulysses* I tried to keep close to fact," the word connotes just this, a satiric force that derides our illusions.[23] Dickens insisted that *Little Dorrit*, his most comprehensive satire, was grounded in fact. Johnson at his most satiric, in "The Vanity of Human Wishes," warns that death mocks our ambitions. Death is a fact we had better get used to. (With Johnson, who died a few years before the French Revolution, we are close to the origin of the argument that reality mocks *political* ambitions, the implication of such claims being that the opponent suffers from delusion, blinded by his ideas in the manner of a Quixote. If the journalist appeals to the facts, the polemicist explains to us what it is about his opponent's mentality that makes him so oblivious to the real.) Satire, it is said, "provides a statistical view of the world," ranging over "a vast number of persons, objects, and actions,"[24] a judgment certainly true of a poem that invites us to scan all of humanity from China to Peru and heaps up examples with an excess characteristic of the satiric mode. Even the sort of numerical vision of the real that we get in the press has, it seems, a precedent in the satiric art of disillusion.

Add to this that the very topicality claimed by the journalist was once the delight of satire. Aristophanes buzzes with topicality. The satires of Horace are laced with contemporary allusions. Chaucer brings satiric types up-to-date by placing them in "topical situations."[25] Behind *The Rape of the Lock* was the kind of incident that becomes the talk of the town. So topical are the writings of Swift that Adam Smith, commenting only a few decades later, found that "we can not now enter altogether into [their] true spirit."[26] Byron identified *Don Juan* as a satire on the *present* condition of society. The criminals, paupers, madmen, and children who figure in *Little Dorrit*, besides denoting Dickens's interest in the disregarded, convey a certain topical concern, for it was to these groups that reformers of his day wanted to teach the habits of civilization. Bearing in mind that topical also means local, we notice that *Pride and Prejudice*, for all its silence on the issues of the hour, is distinctly local and opens with the talk (the "news") of the village. The narrow compass of the work gauges the concentration of its satiric energy. For that matter, the saints called on in the Miller's Tale are local saints.[27] *Dubliners* is laid out on a virtual street map of the city and informed by the spirit of place, while the great girth of *Ulysses* abounds with local allusions. An all-too-full account of some twenty-four hours in the life of Leopold Bloom, *Ulysses* also recalls us to the root of the word "journalism"—day.

Whatever else it may do, satire "always criticizes, it always distorts, it always entertains."[28] Couldn't the same be said of journalism? That journalism idealizes itself in the same terms as satire, namely as "a perfectly ground and uncompromisingly honest mirror,"[29] even as it shows much the same fondness for caricature—this, too, points to kinship. The very position of observation occupied by journalism seems a satiric legacy. Names like the Spectator, the Observer, in fact the Mirror, that have a good journalistic sound today are like dead metaphors, silent reminders of satiric ways of surveying human affairs— the Spectator recalling, for example, the ass who sees all (in effect a spy, an "intelligencer"); the Observer, Johnson's celestial eye surveying mankind in all its folly; the Mirror, Swift's glass in which beholders see the deformities of everyone but themselves. The mirror has specially rich satiric possibilities. You think of Hamlet holding up the glass to his mother, compelling recognition of her deformities, but also dwelling on his own in the mirror of reflection.[30] Ivan Karamazov, shortly after confronting a derisive reflection of himself, demands that the public at the trial of his brother recognize its own image in the spectacle before it.[31]

Observation in and of itself possesses a certain satiric resonance. In part, what makes the commentary of the archsatirist Thersites so free, so unrestrained in its scorn of the heroic, is his own freedom from every other function but comment. Thersites in effect is pure observer, a student of action rather than an agent himself, a point underscored by his refusal of combat in Act V of *Troilus and Cressida*. (In the *libelles* whose Thersites-like vitriol helped create the climate of opinion for the French Revolution, there is a distinct element of someone on the outside looking in, with all that this implies both of voyeurism and an embittered sense of exclusion.)[32] With his exit from life and flight to the eighth sphere, Chaucer's Troilus becomes an absolute observer, laughing with unmistakably satiric contempt at the vanity of earthly life. Ivan Karamazov, also given to satiric scorn, would like to maintain a position of noninvolvement in the drama in his own family, neither assisting nor preventing the murder of his father, in effect an observer of events.

In view of the link between satire and journalism, or satiric license and freedom of comment, it seems fitting that as soon as we learn that Ivan writes eyewitness journalism we also discover that one of his articles may be entirely sarcastic. With Swift (as later with Orwell) journalism itself becomes an object of satire. "Last week I saw a woman flayed, and you will hardly believe how much it altered her person for the worse."[33] In the matter-of-fact tone of this eyewitness report by the Grub Street Hack is heard something of the note of journalism even today, which is also to say that journalism cultivates the credibility that in Swift is purely a satiric device. Swift's acts of mimicry remind us that the satiric project of holding the mirror up to Nature extends readily to the mirroring of language, our second nature; and that the more telling the resemblance of the reflection to the linguistic original, the more parodic it's likely to become.[34] When the language of another is reproduced in a way that accents its otherness, the act of report turns or returns to satire. (By the same token, the journalistic practice of quoting officials, authorities, experts—all of them prime objects of ridicule, traditionally—is like satire neutralized.) An outdoer even of Swift in the parody of tongues, Joyce mimics a multitude of languages with a sense of "objective" removal from any one of them, as though he surveyed the nations of speech from China to Peru, relativizing them all. "This chaffering allincluding most farraginous chronicle," he calls *Ulysses*.[35] The phrase chronicles the original meaning of satire: a farrago.

*

"It's the ads and side features sell a weekly not the stale news in the official gazette," muses Leopold Bloom, a publicity man—at which point a bit of stale news flashes across his brain: "Queen Anne is dead."[36] According to tradition, Addison made this statement in the *Spectator* well after the Queen's death, and it's because of its unhappy timing that it survived, apparently, as a proverb for news gone flat. But that it did live on in irony for some two hundred years, turned by the wit of tradition into a matchlessly elegant illustration of dullness, means that old news may have its value after all.

What kind of claim does the past make on the present? In some cultures the past possesses a more than temporal priority: those who came before are greater, more heroic than the children of the present. While still alive in Swift's elevation of the ancients over the moderns, this epic sense of the past has not held out against the modern creed of progress. It's possible to argue that without a sense of the past we come unmoored, that without a respect for duration our own commitments shift and dissolve, that just because we have nothing to gain or lose by the dead we learn from them what it is to esteem a thing for its own sake. But by the same token, the past matters for its own sake and not solely for the benefits it may confer on us. The claim of the past on the present begins with the fact that there is a great deal more of it than the present. The claim of the satiric tradition begins with its richness and depth. It was because Dostoevsky was in touch with an ancient tradition of satire—a tradition virtually with the magnitude of a lost continent, in one account—that he was able to capture in his fiction the "throb of the 'real present moment.'"[37] Testimony to the richness and depth of the satiric tradition is that it cannot be characterized in any one way. Variously irreverent, subversive, and fired with moral intention (and in notable cases, including Dostoevsky, all of these together), satire seems to laugh at one-dimensionality itself. Precisely because it does not conform to our fashions and formulas it claims our respect. Ironically, though, this increasingly remote tradition *has* conferred a benefit on us. It helped charter free speech.

Among notable arguments for freedom of the press is one by Trenchard and Gordon, reprinted by the young Benjamin Franklin, reading in part, "GUILT only dreads liberty of speech, which drags it out of its lurking holes, and exposes its deformity and horrour to day-light."[38] The unmasking of pretense, the exposure of vice to ridicule and loathing: this is one of the hallowed offices of satire. In Trenchard and Gordon's affirmation of the virtue of publicity satiric license is on the way to becoming political right. "Deformity" alone, after all, refers us to satire, with its grotesques, twisted shapes, things unnatural; bringing ugliness into full view is itself also a satiric act, as in Swift. So, too, before the institution of liberty of speech the satirist *took* liberties in the form of gratuitous excess and violations of decorum. The "civilizing process" that refined manners, heightened restraint, and moderated the general tone of life is a story of the restriction of such license,[39] and as it happens it was by transforming satire itself into a civilizing influence that another of Swift's contemporaries achieved fame as a kind of daily essayist and censor of manners: Joseph Addison. Whether the advent of critical journalism is traced to the satiric letters of Junius or to the emergence of an opposition press in the same year as *Gulliver's Travels*[40] or indeed to the more decorous *Spectator* of Addison and Steele—for the shapes and moods of satire vary, as befits a tradition alert to the many-sidedness of things—journalism seems linked to satire from its inception.

The easy, semiserious style perfected by Addison advertises the decorum of rational liberty. Others in the satiric tradition are less decorous, more dissonant. In some of the masters, in Chaucer, Rabelais, Swift, Dickens, and arguably both Byron and Joyce, we meet with subversive irreverence as well as moral intention, as though the serious and mocking ends of satire converged in the paradox of the seriocomic. Both gravity and levity run through the satiric tradition, both moralization and the ridicule of preaching and pedantry ("The Marriage of Heaven and Hell," for example, blazing with moral ardor even as it plays with diabolism and derides the morality of the priests). And it may be that the conflict of satiric modes grounds freedom of speech better than any one of the modes themselves, confirming as it does the cardinal satiric insight that no single scheme or viewpoint can possibly encompass the fullness of experience. That truth has more shapes than one, as Milton suggests in his qualified defense of a free press, is itself a truth powerfully enforced by the discordance of the voices of satire, and not only the difference between, say, the urbanity of Horace and the indignation of Juvenal, but the deeper philosophical dissonance between the modes of seriousness and laughter (as in the tonal paradoxes of *Don Juan*). In the manner of the seriocomic, Chaucer never really reconciles "solaas" and "sentence" in the *Canterbury Tales*, the unparliamentary debates of the *Tales* presenting perhaps as pure an example of free discussion as any in literature. Though Chaucer belongs in the first instance to the tradition of estates satire citing the duties, and therefore also the defections from duty, of the several ranks in a hierarchical society, he has strong ties with the ancient Menippea where ranks are leveled and every convention of decorum violated. In the tradition of Chaucer are authors as far apart as Addison, in his capacity as a light satirist, and Joyce, his multiple narration in *Ulysses* a reminder of the sheer manyness of the *Canterbury Tales* and his heroine a "metempsychosis" of the Wife of Bath. (That Chaucer, who plays no part in Joyce's Homeric-Shakespearean "system," should nevertheless find resonance in *Ulysses* seems a comment on the narrowness of system itself.) In the verbatim transcript of Molly Bloom's inner speech the pretense of faithful report that runs through the English novel attains an ironic fulfillment, and the satiric potential that was always present in the disclaimer of fiction, from Chaucer on, is mined to its depths.

The term "satire" derives from the word for medley or miscellany and, ultimately, as I've noted, that for full; hence, "satiety." Satire is sometimes called by critics a farrago, a term used by Juvenal: *"Quidquid agunt homines . . . nostri est farrago libelli."* Later adopted by Steele as a motto for the *Tatler*, Juvenal's proclamation—"Whatever men do . . . forms the motley subject of my book"—reads like the original of "All the news that's fit to print."[41] In the satiric tradition there is special emphasis on "all" both in the sense of matter above and beyond the narrowly fit and proper, and in the sense of a sprawling variety. The plenitude of Chaucer, and of his successors Dickens and Joyce, measures the meaning of "all." What is now the journalist's maxim was once the satirist's, as the daily practice of telling all was once a satiric privilege. In the breadth and abundance of satire, with its writ to survey "whatever men do," the spirit as distinct from the formal right of free speech is realized.

As might be imagined, in the satiric tradition excess takes a variety of shapes; to cite but a few, the surplus of detail and allusion in *Ulysses* as well as the richness of both of the Blooms, over and beyond anything enjoyed by their satiric forebears; the crowding of the Dickens world; the excess of innuendo in Jane Austen; the liberty of comment in *Don Juan,* Byron's survey of all things and then some;[42] the acclamation of excess as such in "The Marriage of Heaven and Hell"; the overintensity of satire itself in Swift;[43] the endless suggestiveness of *Don Quixote;* the gigantism of Rabelais. Hamlet's famous surplus of consciousness might be read as an example of satiric excess, the result of subjecting himself to the same kind of scourging exposure to which he subjects others. So it is that "his self-consciousness exceeds his role and blocks his performance of it."[44] On the comic side, antifeminist satire produces its own scourge in the Wife of Bath, whose excess is such that she overfulfills the role of wife, having married five times. Exaggeration seems dear to satire in general, as though only too much were enough. In it is such a wealth of potential, in fact, that different schools of belief have drawn on it, binding up its power in the language of doctrine.

Consumer society is in its own way a hymn to excess, a never-ending dream of satiety, a running gloss on that proverb of Hell, "You never know what is enough unless you know what is more than enough," and like satire, it too is a hash, as a glance at any magazine rack or television listing confirms. Consumer culture spills over into ridicule of itself, its excess taking the form of a kind of continual exposé of its own productions. There is also a critical style where the human face seems locked in a smirk, satiric by force of habit, without knowing why, satiric even at its own expense. This sort of advanced mockery seems the very note of a consumer economy that joins the production and destruction of value in a single act. I would argue that in the final analysis consumer culture is satiric only in the sense that its cynicism, by ridiculing its own products, clears the way for new ones just as consumer goods per se are used up, discarded, and replenished. Satire, in other words, is reduced to an instrument of the economic process, serving to speed up the production and consumption of cultural goods and ensuring that nothing stands too securely or too long. Historically satire has performed a less menial role. As I have argued, it has given life to freedom of speech, inspiring the play of voices in Chaucer, the swordwork of Dickens even within the constraints of sentimental fiction, the unheard-of liberties of Rabelais, Swift, Joyce, the fantastic truth of Orwell. In the postreticent society journalism loses memory of (is "emancipated" from) its historical sources, even as the shock and excess once belonging to satire become daily routine.

A word connoting the most direct and least artful presentation of infor-mation, journalism burgeoned in England, as we know, during the golden age of the literary hoax. Both Swift and Defoe, each for his own ends, pass off their fictions as authentic accounts. Lending them what is called credibility is a certain flatness of tone, an aspect of literal notation, as though the style of factual report perfected itself as fiction. Now the author posing as nothing of the kind is one guise of the "eiron" who pretends to be less than he is. This study traces some vectors of influence from a poet who took that posture habitually and whose greatest work, in fact, rests on a pretense of verbatim report. In the *Canterbury Tales* Chaucer is the ass who sees all, the observer who himself goes all but unobserved, the mirror of folly. As the most journalistic of novelists, Defoe brings out the sibling relation of the novel and reportage. Even his work, however, has a Chaucerian precedent, Moll Flanders recalling that other five-times-married woman of enterprise, the Wife of Bath. "It was past flourishing time with me when I might expect to be courted for a mistress; that agreeable part had declin'd some time, and the ruins only appear'd of what had been. . . ."[45]

Joyce in turn was a rapt reader of Defoe, whom he admired as founder of the English novel, mage of the real, and creator of "the unique, the incomparable" Moll Flanders.[46] Unique and incomparable, and yet a second coming of the Wife of Bath. With a conventionality odd in him, Joyce took Defoe as an original who worked without literary models and Chaucer as a derivative who followed now the courtly model and now the *Decameron*. In point of fact, as I'll argue, it was the Wife of Bath whom Joyce effectually brought to life as he returned to the very springs of freedom. The hyperrealism of Joyce recalls the protorealism of Chaucer, the unedited speech of Molly Bloom the streaming monologue of the Wife.

In looking into the satiric foundations of journalism, then, I begin with Chaucer. Chaucer poses as a reporter in and of the *Canterbury Tales*, enacting his fictitious role in a way that proved to have the greatest cultural resonance. Once known as the father of English poetry, Chaucer is certainly a force on English prose. If Addison's influence was such that he contributed to the construction of the modern public realm, his role as a "Spectator" and the style, at once tolerant and critical, in which he performed it are both Chaucerian. And from Addison a line of sorts extends to the also tolerant and critical Trollope, whose prose, implying more than it quite says, is among the most finely tuned expressions of Victorian reticence. (Even reticence, however, can be an expression of satiric liberty. The silence of Jane Austen on the most pressing public questions of her day is itself, perhaps, a way of saying more by saying less.) But much as the European novel in general presents two lines, one concerned with propriety of tone, the other consciously discordant, so a second Chaucer tradition almost in the nature of a double shadows the first—one in which the dimness of Chaucer's modest persona becomes the stone-blindness of Swift's reasonable man offering a modest proposal to a journal-reading public; in which Chaucerian plenty becomes the profusion of satiric types beyond any narrative requirement in Dickens; and the diverse narration of the pilgrims on their journey to Canterbury becomes the shattered narrative decorum of *Ulysses*.[47] From Chaucer to Joyce: reflection on the practice of framing leads Bakhtin to a discussion of *Eugene Onegin* as a living encyclopedia where the "varied and opposing voices" of the era mix.[48] The *Canterbury Tales* are framed, and *Ulysses*, as a kind of auditory horn of plenty, possesses just the encyclopedism Bakhtin describes; for that matter, so do the *Tales* themselves.[49] When *Ulysses* was admitted into the United States, the judge in effect adopted the argument put forward by Chaucer in his "journalistic" apology for the indecorousness of the *Canterbury Tales*. When Orwell, with strong ties to the Joyce-Dickens-Swift line, both summed up and transcended his work as a journalist in *Nineteen Eighty-four*, he made use of a literary form well known to Chaucer: Menippean satire. (In Bakhtin's account, Menippean satire was instrumental in getting literature to speak of the present moment, in contrast with the legendary past, in the first place. Hence its designation as journalistic.) The second Chaucer tradition, indeed, seems to flow from the Menippean Chaucer, the first the Chaucer of estates satire. Both pick up the device of reporting, with Trollope, for example, depicting the everyday life of the more comfortable classes in the mid–Victorian era with the trustworthiness of "a faithful reporter," albeit in a Chaucerian tone varying from sarcasm to sympathy,[50] and Joyce removing all signs of authorial intrusion from the soliloquy of Molly Bloom, as though perfecting Chaucer's pretense of reporting words exactly as they were uttered. The newspaper itself Joyce took as the "principal emblem of modern capitalism . . . wasting the spirit with its persistent attacks upon the integrity of the word, narcotizing its readers with superficial facts, habituating them to secular and clerical authority."[51]

As I will try to show, the first of the Chaucer lines—possessed of an estates mentality, however qualified—moderates scorn and ridicule in one degree or another while still exercising the liberty of satire. Addison tempers ridicule with humility and expresses himself without ostentation even while playing the role of satirist-general. Austen and Trollope too have a style midway between levity and gravity, and both raise the lack of ostentation into a kind of rhetoric of reticence. (Trollope, we might say, is an Addisonian both by temperament and by way of Jane Austen. As a young man he had already decided "that *Pride and Prejudice* was the best novel in the English language.")[52] Generally speaking, the first line keeps away from the rudeness and rancor that are part of the heritage of satire, yet claims liberties conferred by satire as a traditional institution. The second line indulges the excess of satire even at the expense of the first. Hence Swift's satire on the voice of public spirit, like Addison's, which became the official voice of modern journalism; hence Dickens's immoderation and Joyce's overthrow of the Victorian norms of which Trollope is the symbol. To measure the gap between the two lines we might set Byron's use of the common style in *Don Juan*, the better to instruct his readers in the elements of style and "civil behavior,"[53] against Addison's course in the elements of style and civility. Each line in its own way, however, harks back to Chaucer in his role as reporter of the *Canterbury Tales*, and both seem to assert the priority of satire over its offshoot.

The second Chaucer line, I have suggested, is Menippean. For "Menippea" Northrop Frye proposes the less arcane "anatomy," implying dissection of a subject. When Dickens dreams of a magazine specializing in the "anatomisation of humbug,"[54] the term calls up the General Prologue of the *Canterbury Tales*, which is just that; but also the anatomical inspection of the human animal in *Gulliver's Travels* and even the keying of *Ulysses* to the organs of the human body. Magnetic groupings like this indicate the force of a tradition. Now if an anatomy presents a "comprehensive survey of human life" in satiric terms,[55] like the overview of society in the *Canterbury Tales*, this is perhaps one more indication that the critical survey of the human scene was a satiric practice before it became a journalistic one. Dickens did anatomize sham—in satire. At the core of his anatomy of society *Little Dorrit* is the issue of circumlocution, a strangely willful act that reads like a perversion of freedom of speech. It is satire itself that recoups the freedom tangled up in circumlocution; and among the voices of verbosity satirized in *Little Dorrit* is the press.

Within the second Chaucer tradition *Ulysses* seems to possess special resonance. Curiously, also, within *Ulysses* itself the two traditions cross and recross like the lines of the novel in Bakhtin's account.[56] They cross in the persons of Bloom and Stephen, the first a benevolent middlebrow of a Lockean cast, and like Addison a kind of publicist, the second an intensely sardonic voice closer to Addison's mighty opposite Swift. A meeting between Bloom and Stephen may be destined, but a meeting of their minds seems destined, in spite of their affinities, not to come off. If Bloom moves in the orbit of journalism, and keeps his quips to himself, Stephen speaks in the voice of satire. (As he begins to deliver the parable of the plums, Stephen exhorts himself, "On now. Dare it," meaning roughly, "Say what you know." As satirist he is in touch with the spirit of free speech. Bloom says a lot less than he knows.)[57] Something of the estranged relation between satire and journalism investigated in this study is figured in the failed encounter between a man of enlightened benevolence, which is the moral tone of the better sort of journalism to this day, and a youth of caustic retorts to whom he means little.

*

Consumer society bears a radical hostility to cultural memory, an attitude reinforced by journalism's fixation on the present moment.[58] A constant theme of consumer culture, in fact, is that we have been emancipated from the lies and bonds of the past—that we are free to fly where those before us walked in darkness—that it is our fortune to live in the first society on earth where people can do and have and be what they like. All but officially repudiated is the traditional sentiment that the past is the ground of the present. In the satiric traditions considered here, it is otherwise. One line enacts a kind of symbolic return to origins, with Swift, for example, urging us back to the plain terms of the Father's will in *A Tale of a Tub*—a project akin to the republican myth of the renewal of virtue, except that Swift's emphasis falls on the disease of degeneracy rather than the cure. Dickens, also a reformer, dreams of a return to the apostolic simplicity of the heart. Joyce returns in *Ulysses* to the very headwaters of fiction, at the same time renewing the original meaning of "journalism" as the account of a day, while Orwell found that only by going back to the satiric origins of journalism could he do justice to the monstrous novelty of the totalitarian state. The boldness of Orwell's satire in *Nineteen Eighty-four* affiliates him with a "journalistic genre of antiquity" that he may have had no acquaintance with at first hand. With Addison, of the other line, it is the other way around: by affiliating himself with a classical tradition he accredits his satiric role, reduced as it is. Attaching classical tags to his essays that not only dignify the papers of a day with an aspect of permanence but credential the practice of commenting critically on whatever men do, Addison finds in Horace, especially, precedent for his own liberties. The Addisonians too are oriented to the past, if less inclined to a sharp break with existing practice. Though looking to the ancients, Addison does not reject the present in favor of the past but secures the gains of the recent Revolution in the hope of making another unlikely. Jane Austen's conspicuous silence on the issues of the day in a revolutionary era may well attest her preference for the traditional institution of satire over the upstart, journalism. An attachment to established institutions places Trollope at variance with "the way we live now." (In spite of the topical immediacy of its title, *The Way We Live Now* takes after a work of thirty years before, *Vanity Fair*.)[59] In contrast with a journalism that knows only the present, both of these traditions, though themselves at variance, are grounded in the past.

There isn't much, I imagine, that Joyce and Trollope would agree on, but both envision the journalist as vulgarian, one who robes himself in the importance of a profession that has now arrived like him. Full of himself, windy, manifestly insincere, Ignatius Gallaher in "A Little Cloud" so overplays the man of the world that the failed Little Chandler looks almost good by contrast, and so celebrates his own legend that the reader of *Ulysses* can't help wondering how big he blew the story of his exploit in 1882 that the editor Myles Crawford now tells as his own. And just as the editor's vision of the past seems inflated with falsity, so Gallaher's affected nostalgia for "the old country," "old times," and "the old gang" in "A Little Cloud" establishes him beyond doubt as a parvenu. Journalism itself is like a parvenu in this, at least, that it throws the past in the shadows. Yet even the word "report," with its root meaning of carrying back, conveys some impression of repetition and return. "Report" in Lucian and Swift suggests the act of bringing back a sort of cargo of tales from across the sea. The motif of wandering and return is of course strongly inscribed in *Ulysses*, whose last episode has Molly Bloom—herself a kind of return of the also nostalgic Wife of Bath—thinking of "the dear deaead days beyondre call."[60] Satire is rich in recall, both nostalgic and parodic; indeed, a parody is bound to its original by its own sort of nostalgia for origins. The commemoration of the mythic past in *Ulysses* is a uniquely ironic instance of the tropism to the past shown in satire as a whole. Even Lucian seems to have an affection for Homer. The first order of business in Byron's magnum opus is to dismiss the specious new heroes that fill "the gazettes" in favor of "our ancient friend Don Juan."

Indeed, regardless of their several leanings, all of the satirists discussed in this study possess an orientation to the past simply by virtue of membership in a tradition. I call satire a tradition rather than a genre because if a genre is a category of literary works more or less defined by a set of formal conditions, then satire is altogether too loose, too unconstrained formally, to qualify. Satire runs in drama and narrative, in poetry and prose, in the extravagance of the Menippea (which likes to use both) and the order-bound tradition of the estates, and in fact in literary "forms," from the short essay to the long novel, where the requirements of form itself are relaxed. Satire resembles a genre in perhaps one respect only, that it too possesses memory—a fact attested by the continual evocation of precursors by the satirists in this study. The freedom of their speech, it seems to me, reflects not only the independence of set forms enjoyed by satire as such but the richness of the inheritance they claim.

Journalism, on the other hand, works on the premise that each day is a new one and that its own history has nothing to do with its task of delivering the news. The irony is that in sloughing off the past and proclaiming its independence of all the traditions of narrative, journalism creates a product more completely generic—more predictable and formulaic, more lacking in the unique—than anything known to the tradition of satire itself. While the plain repetition that marks journalism as a whole reflects the influence of technology, in a larger sense the generic packaging and content of the news are a sign of sheer impoverishment—the loss of cultural capital and substance with the rejection of the past. Where "history" means what is dead and done with, the news of the day takes on the character of a standard consumer good that is itself destined to be done with in short order. Emancipation from the past, a past now portrayed as a long spell of darkness, gives rise in the consumer society to a stereotypy new in degree and kind. During the Chinese Cultural Revolution the campaign against old thought produced a standardization of language so severe that not only newspapers and posters but teapots, spittoons, towels, and tickets were printed with identical messages.[61] In consumer society the campaign against the past takes the form not of a spasm of riotous discipline but a continuous derogation all the more effective because not ordered from above. To conservatives the French Revolution illustrated a cosmic law of perverse effects decreeing that attempts at liberty are bound to end in despotism.[62] No such law is known to the human mind, although the self-defeating nature of folly is indeed a cardinal theme of satire. What can be said is that casting off the burden of the past, even if it makes us freer, may leave us poorer.

A fictional case in point concerns the apothecary and freelance journalist of *Madame Bovary*, champion of "the immortal principles of eighty-nine," whose every statement frames one of those received ideas that were Flaubert's aversion. Assailing darkness and superstition like some Voltaire of papier-mâché, Homais speaks with a flagrant unoriginality that marks the author's concern with the mass production of ideas themselves. Convinced as he is of the path to human freedom, Homais can only repeat his phrases in a mechanical way that belies the quality of freedom. Homais is the human embodiment of ideas more generic than genre itself. In allowing this publicist the utmost freedom to damn himself with his own words, Flaubert effectively turns the tables on journalism by subjecting it to the tradition from which it came—a tradition that Homais, in his animus against the past, has forgotten.

At once comical and shameless in his magnification of himself, Homais establishes the figure of the journalist as vulgarian. Joyce, a disciple of Flaubert, re-creates the type in Ignatius Gallaher in *Dubliners*. (Its very ethos of precise notation seems to pull this work in a satiric direction.) On the other side of the tree, Trollope gives us Quintus Slide in *The Prime Minister*, in his impudence posturing like a tribune of the People.[63] Similar in spirit is the portrayal of the scandalmonger George Flack in Henry James's *The Reverberator*, an exposé of the new journalism of the 1880s. Here what I have called the generic quality of journalistic ideas is made over to the reporter:

> He was not a particular person, but a sample or memento—reminding one of certain "goods" for which there is a steady popular demand. You would scarcely have expected him to have a name other than that of his class: a number, like that of the day's newspaper, would have been the most that you could count on, and you would have expected vaguely to find the number high—somewhere up in the millions.[64]

This lack of distinction extends, moreover, to others in *The Reverberator*. Mr. Dosson is a zero, an absentee, as lacking as his own sense of the past, and the heroine less a character than a vacancy. (Among the party of those injured by the reporter is one Mme de Cliché.) Of Dosson, adrift in a kind of normalized amnesia, it is said that he felt an "absence of precedents" for events.[65] In depicting the press in the person of Flack as a force that nullifies the past and resounds through empty cultural space—in exposing the cult of the exposé—James too subjects journalism to its own precedent, satire.

Journalism in turn tends to unwrite the memory of its own satiric sources. In order to maintain steady demand for a product whose attractions might otherwise wear out, journalism trumpets the events of the day. Accordingly, from banner headlines to epic labels like "the trial of the century," a sort of rhetoric of inflation runs through the press, proclaiming that things have never been of more urgent interest, of more critical import, than at this moment. In itself the hyperbolization of the present is enough to block memory of something as traditional as satire—all the more because satire likes to deflate our self-importance. Think only of the depiction of the war between the Russians and the Turks by Homais's own mentor Voltaire, in *Micromégas*, as an encounter between mites swollen with ideas of their own grandeur and the justice of their cause. Events great from one perspective may appear in the eye of satire a contemptible farce.[66] The humbling of human pretense at work here—and this is but one example of a general satiric policy—is not only foreign but inconceivable to journalism as we know it. If journalism has its sources in satire as I suppose, then like many another modern it has forgotten its own roots.

No doubt the erosion of memory in the consumer society has obscured the satiric foundations of journalism. Not only have those foundations been forgotten, however. They have been built over.

Along with the derogation of the past in the consumer society goes the consignment of the very word "morality" to the past. ("Ethics" is more acceptable because more modernistic in sound.) "Morality" is a relic, a vestige of the same Comstockery responsible for the repression of modern art on one hand and sex on the other: so goes a main theme of consumer culture, almost as if the Victorian struggle against the past in the name of progress had been transformed into a struggle against the Victorians themselves. A necessary loser in this transaction is satire, if only because satire even at its freest is charged with moral intention. Who can deny that Gargantua's letter to his son, Blake's treatment of priests and pedants, Joyce's depiction of fanaticism and intolerance, are so animated? O'Brien in *Nineteen Eighty-four* is priest and pedagogue in one, more fanatical, more intolerant, than any mere bigot, the announcer of a new dark age. Those to whom morality connotes nothing more than repression and cultural darkness have lost touch with satire altogether.

If the word "morality" has gone out of favor, key words of satire like "folly" and "knavery" have been displaced by other terms for the reality under the mask of appearance; this too must contribute to the loss of satire's cultural position. Whether in the spirit of Marxism it discerns class interest under the deceptions of appearance, or in the spirit of psychology tangles of anxiety and the confused stirrings of the true self, the postsatiric vocabulary fills the place of folly and knavery with terms claiming more scientific status.[67] Additionally, satire seems to have an affinity with stoicism that puts it at variance with the tenor of our age. The deflation of human pretense is after all a stoic project as much as a satiric one. Horace's beliefs are stoic at core. Probably Chaucer's private sentiments were in tune with the *Consolation of Philosophy*—a mix of prose and verse in the Menippean tradition—which he translated. (Troilus's sardonic view of human folly from the serenity of the eighth sphere is like the comprehensive survey of society in the *Canterbury Tales*, but in a stoic key.) Both the impiously satiric Voltaire and the piously satiric Johnson espoused stoicism. The satiric streak in Adam Smith goes along with a neo-Roman stoicism. Jane Austen's prose finds its freedom in self-restraint, as though in accord with a stoic ethos. The reduced, phlegmatic tone of Orwell might be understood as a kind of stoicism past its time. Leopold Bloom's feeling for "the apathy of the stars" helps mark him a child of the Enlightenment.[68] But stoic dispassion has dropped from the scheme of our experience even as the ideal of professional detachment has risen to prestige. The "cool, unemotional and hence skeptical" survey of the human scene practiced in the Augustan age, at the noon of satire,[69] has itself been professionalized. It has become the professed ethos of journalism.

CHAPTER 1

Chaucer and the
Rehearsal of Voices

A comic playing with languages, a story 'not from the author' (but from a narrator, posited author or character), character speech, character zones and lastly various introductory or framing genres are the basic forms for incorporating and organizing heteroglossia in the novel."[1] How is it that Bakhtin seems to be talking about the *Canterbury Tales*, which isn't a novel at all? Perhaps because no one has caught with such lucidity as Chaucer the moment that so fascinates Bakhtin—the point when plurality appears, when, in the words of another, "previously isolated strata begin to communicate with one another" and "diverse conceptions of the world" mingle and collide and things cease to be self-evident.[2] Bakhtin sets "dialogue," understood as a process openended, dissonant, inconclusive, against all that is fixed and finished.[3] Even in spite of being capped by the Parson's Tale, the Canterbury contest strikes us as dialogical in just this sense. The tales offer diverse views of the world—views attached not to characters in the modern understanding of the term, but to what I call voices.

*

The entry to the *Canterbury Tales* is by way of a framing narrative portraying pilgrims from many walks of life who happen to meet in a London tavern. Drawn by a narrator enchanted with externals and lacking in comprehension, and not Chaucer though bearing his name, these portraits are nevertheless flecked with the sharp if implicit perceptions of the poet himself. Among those we meet, and somehow characteristic, are a Prioress who isn't quite a Prioress and a Wife not currently married. Evidently we have entered a realm Bakhtin would call novelistic, where people are not equal to their given role (so that in *The Brothers Karamazov* Dmitri is a *former* military officer, Alyosha

22

not exactly a novice, Ivan a *sometime* journalist), a realm of sharp questioning and satiric vision. The "surplus" found in such figures—another expression of satiric excess—reappears at another level in the sheer multitude of the pilgrims themselves.[4] Later the pilgrims, a good many of them, are brought to life and granted their moment to say what they will and vex one another. The impression conveyed by the *Canterbury Tales* is accordingly a diversity of voices—not exactly a babel, but not a chorus either. Distinguished by a rich plenitude, the *Tales* seem to be in touch with satire's root meaning of variety. As Dryden, himself a theorist of satire, wrote of the *Canterbury Tales*, "here is God's plenty."

An inconspicuous observer of his fellow pilgrims, Chaucer recalls Lucius, the socially invisible but observant ass whose lone consolation was "that my long ears could pick up conversations at a great distance."[5] The material of the *Canterbury Tales* bears a certain affinity to Apuleius and evokes vividly the wealth of the satiric tradition that lies buried under journalism as we know it. The reporter's pose assumed by Chaucer in the *Canterbury Tales*—that is to say, his adoption of a lowly and asslike role far beneath that of a poet—is itself a satiric pretense.

The portraits in the General Prologue place us in a hierarchical universe where everyone in principle occupies an assigned position with fixed duties. In principle, because one like the Wife of Bath—all at once widow, wife, and whore—confounds the very notion of an assigned position; while one like the Friar makes an occupation of betraying his duty. Practice does not conform with theory, although this reflects on the person and not the position itself, Monk and not monkhood. In accordance with estates satire the members of the various orders of a corporate society are judged, at least implicitly, by the ideal of their role. In the tales themselves, as the pilgrims pass from objects of description to voices in their own right, the reader seems to pass from estates satire to something more freewheeling. Here too practice fails to conform with theory: with the drunken Miller's insistence on telling his tale out of turn, the Host's plan for an orderly succession of tales hits the rocks, and in fact the chain of being that authorizes the ending of the Knight's Tale, and underwrites the social hierarchy of the General Prologue itself, is sharply parodied in the chain of descent from that tale to the Miller's and the Reeve's. But once the Miller lances the Knight, the reader can only think it's a good thing that practice doesn't conform to plan. Evidently the tales themselves stand on a different basis from the General Prologue; as I will propose, from the former flows a tradition of satiric license and excess, from the latter a tradition of more decorous social criticism.[6] The hinge of the whole would seem to be the shift in Chaucer's role from the speaker of the General Prologue to the recorder of the tales, and it is at just this point, probably with an eye on the Miller's Tale, that he issues a strategic apology.

Bringing into being such different voices as we hear in the *Canterbury Tales* and giving them the power to contest each other meant taking liberties with gentility. And in order to secure his audience's indulgence, Chaucer not only screened himself behind an endearingly dim-witted persona but offered an apology to the effect that he had no choice—he had to report the words of churls like the Miller just as they were delivered. He had to report them verbatim.

> For this ye knowen al so wel as I,
> Whoso shal telle a tale after a man,
> He moot reherce as ny as evere he kan
> Everich a word, if it be in his charge,
> Al speke he nevere so rudeliche and large,
> Or ellis he moot telle his tale untrewe.[7]

Evidently Chaucer is preparing for the moment when the flotsam of the pilgrimage, the clowns, knaves, and fools, make themselves heard. How else, he seems to say, could these have spoken except like the types they are? Further, how could a fool's exhibition of his own folly be taken as anything but a reflection on himself? But of course the very existence of all those whose words the poet reports so faithfully is a fiction. Though the Elizabethans seem to have believed the Canterbury pilgrimage had a basis in fact—this even as they looked to Chaucer as the source of English poetry[8]—the poet's original audience must have understood that his pose as a reporter of the words of others was just that. The pose authorizes Chaucer's departure from courtly style, his expansion of the range of speech (always assuming the sufferance of the audience). It is a holiday propriety that delivers the words of rogues in a style "proper" to them, although such purely dramatic fitness proved good enough for Dryden and would eventually, in the *Ulysses* decision, be recognized in law.[9] Anyway, when journalists today cite their responsibility to report the facts, they little imagine they follow after a poet whose facts were an invention. The satirist's alibi has become the journalist's watchword. Even plain fact, the rock of the journalistic profession, has something of a satiric intention about it in the *Canterbury Tales*. Among the performances disclaimed by the poet as though they weren't his invention in the first place is that of the Miller, whose tale burlesques the Knight's romance (an opposition that sets the course for

the *Canterbury Tales* as a whole).[10] Studded with realistic details like a smith
working overtime—marking the day of the week and the time of the day
where the Knight's Tale stretched indefinitely over years—the Miller's Tale
endows fact itself with an element of satiric assertion.

Consider first the notation of time in the Miller's Tale, so different from
the vague epic past of the tale preceding. "On a Saterday" Nicholas constructs
his plot against John and takes to his room. By sundown the next day the
landlord has begun to worry. After his servant peering in at the cat-hole—a
characteristic detail—discovers Nicholas in a trance, the student is roused;
whereupon John learns that "a Monday next, at quarter night" God will send a
second flood. The water will recede "about pryme upon the next day." On
Monday, meanwhile, as the carpenter races to get the survival craft built,
Absolon inquires after him in Oseneye, where he has twice before been placed.
As the tricks of the tale are played out, timing is all. The comic catastrophe is the
product not of human design, still less of Providence, but of a clash of designs
and finally the fortune of the moment. That the catastrophe takes place at a
given time, at a given place, matters as much as the hot iron that is its instrument
or the passion of revenge that inspires the now furious priest. Suddenly all the
elements of circumstance—all the points on the journalistic checklist, from
why to how—come into their own. In the brilliant staging of the tale's finale
all figure, and figure with a kind of stark equality, as though a fact were a fact.
Just as the Miller levels the pilgrimage itself by talking back to the Knight
in defiance of the Host's design, so his tale reduces method and motive, time
and place, even wit and luck, to a single satiric level of significance. It's fitting,
too, that such marked circumstantial detail should appear in a context of satire,
considering that from a point of view fixed on "timeless universals," particulars
have something derisory about them. (Far from mirroring something timeless,
the Miller celebrates an outcome so fortuitous, a dovetailing of factors so
unusual, it can happen precisely once.) If Chaucer's burlesques play off against
the norms of courtliness, the satiric portrayal of the mechanics of circumstance
in the Miller's Tale presupposes the traditional bias (as in the Knight's Tale)
against such practicalities.

Among the tools of reduction, notes Kenneth Burke, are "the atomistic
vocabularies that would account for entities in terms of the particles of which
they are thought to be composed, as one might account for a building in terms
of the materials used in its construction."[11] The fabliau presents a reductive
vision of human life, specially reductive in the case of the Chaucerian fabliau
breaking action itself down into its particles or minimum elements. With this
in mind we can perhaps make some sense of Nicholas's absurdly contrived and

indirect method of gaining an end, union with Alisoun, that is his to begin with. The needless complication of Nicholas's scheme brings the logistical factor into play—activates, as it were, the reductive effect of the fabliau. How to get John to work himself to exhaustion; when the tubs, those reduced arks, are to be constructed, and where hung—issues like these suddenly become material. Through Nicholas's machinations, and their unforeseen result when they run into another's, the satiric vision of the fabliau is realized.

In Chaucer's hands, indeed, the fabliau is concerned as perhaps no other literary form had ever been with the sheer logistics of events. When Absolon is given his kiss; where moonlight streams in through Symkyn's wall; why his wife is up and about; how May maneuvers her husband—all is duly noted. The factuality of these tales is the measure of their satiric force. In fabliaux like these—each alive with detail and brilliantly disenchanted, as though Chaucer had realized the full potential of the genre itself—an event is stripped down to the elements of who, what, when, where, why, and how. Perhaps these tales can therefore be taken as a satiric precedent of the news story and its reductions, much as the subversion of fictions of gentility in the fabliaux would be translated into daily practice by a press defying the conventions of reticence. In any case there is a strong sense of the here and now about many of Chaucer's fabliaux, an impression enhanced by their use of current idioms.[12] The Miller's Tale is set emphatically in modern Oxford, in contrast with the prior tale set in ancient Greece, and its details check out.[13] Also modern and authentically local, the Reeve's Tale in addition turns on the location of a cradle. The Shipman's Tale of bargaining, both sexual and financial, takes place in a disenchanted present at the other pole from the "long ago and far away" of romance. And it is the fabliaux, presumably, that call forth the "reporter's" apology in the General Prologue.

If the _Canterbury Tales_ in all their discordant plenitude are really an act of poetic license, why didn't Chaucer just _claim_ poetic license rather than encircling his text with disclaimers and apologies? A stranger to the rhetoric of rights, Chaucer is loath to claim a privilege not accorded by his audience (and as a political man he must have had a keen sense of the compact between patron and client). Nor in any case was it his practice to claim for himself the originality of authorship. Self-diminution was his habit. In his pose as a copyist there is even a certain semblance of truth in that he freely borrowed, but also freely transformed, narrative material. If, as Bakhtin claims, the genius of European prose was "born and shaped in the process of a free (that is, reformulating) translation of others' works," this was the way of Chaucer, whose most original creations, the Wife of Bath and the Pardoner, were derived from preexisting models.[14] While the fabliau pictures a kind of present-tense world where tradition casts no shadow (hence its brilliance and flatness), Chaucer as poet always seems to ground his work on something already in existence, something proven, as it were, finding in the work of other hands the ways and means of his art. Above all Chaucer borrowed from Boccaccio. How ironic then that Boccaccio, who certainly qualified for the honors of authorship, struck the same journalistic pose as Chaucer himself.

In the conclusion to the *Decameron*, anticipating criticism of his work, Boccaccio replies that had he expurgated his tales he would have betrayed his duty to report words as he heard them. "I could do nothing but write down the tales as they were told, and if those people who had told them had told them more beautifully, I should have written them more beautifully," he alleges, disclaiming his own invention like Chaucer.[15] Here then is a purely satiric original of the claim to be telling the ugly truth that became a sort of ritual of journalistic "realism" beginning in the early decades of this century, a line of defense that has itself been reproduced almost photographically from one instance to the next in the name of innovation.[16] Anyway, far from copying down the words of pilgrims, it would seem Chaucer was following the example and reformulating the words of Boccaccio in casting himself as a reporter at all.[17]

Following Chaucer's apology for the liberties of the *Canterbury Tales* comes the election of the Host, Harry Bailly, as lord of the pilgrimage. Just as freedom of speech has a precedent in Chaucerian satire, so does the practice of election now associated with it (and still the occasion for slanging contests and public caricature). While even the most despotic regime today claims to represent the will of the people, the theory of consent dates back only to the seventeenth century, when its novelty was met with derision in some quarters. "Would they send men about to poll the whole nation?" wrote a critic of Locke.[18] In the Tabard Inn all thirty of the pilgrims are polled, agreeing by a unanimous show of hands, and in a pure example of the consent of the governed, to be "reuled" in all things by their Host, Harry Bailly (General Prologue, l. 816). The election of Harry by acclamation bears traces of the rites of ridicule described by Bakhtin in his study of the medieval culture of laughter, rites including the election of mock kings on St. Valentine's Day, the setting for Chaucer's *Parliament of Fowls*.[19] In the theory of consent that finds official expression in Locke such satiric content drops away. His popularizer Addison softens satire itself even while enacting the Harry Bailly–like role of the critic whose judgments his own electors agree to follow in matters "heigh and lough" (General Prologue, l. 817).

*

The Chaucer persona doesn't only report the *Canterbury Tales* but reports *on* the pilgrims who tell them. And in this case as it happens he repeats the words of others, with or without an awareness of doing so. Laced with direct perceptions that obscure their largely secondhand character, the portraits in the General Prologue combine almost indistinguishably the kinds of things the pilgrims might say about themselves, things that might typically be said about them by admiring others, and things they wouldn't want said at all. Perhaps our reporter, with his sense of being an average man, feels that if these elements are mixed up completely enough, a balanced view results. In any event it seems to me that the descriptive technique of the General Prologue can be taken in different directions: satires on fools and knaves who don't realize their true character is on view; novels in which a narrator slips in and out of a character's perspective or makes comments now sympathetic, now critical; or finally journalism itself, which seems to flatten out the ironized language that enabled modern prose and erase its "faint smile."[20]

It was in response to the rise of journalism, in the broad sense that includes not just news but the general merchandising of ideas, that Swift perfected the device of getting some man of ideas to hold forth and expose his mania. The trick goes back to Lucian's way of allowing speakers to condemn themselves with their own words, a tactic that has been called black journalism.[21] As it happens, the two most compelling figures on the Canterbury pilgrimage, the Wife of Bath and the Pardoner, condemn themselves with their own words—she as a compendium of the most infamous traits of her sex, he as an exploiter of ignorance and credulity—but in a way that distinguishes them from a mere type of vice. It's as if the freedom conferred by the chance to speak, rather than to be described or spoken *of* as in the General Prologue, gave them the means and power to contest their own definition. In the same tradition is Molly Bloom, who when she finally gets the floor speaks with such effect that she cannot possibly be reduced to a satiric function or an author's ploy.

In the shift from the General Prologue, which is *about* the pilgrims, to the tales themselves, presented by the several pilgrims in their own right, the principle of polyphony as Bakhtin sets it forth in his study of Dostoevsky is practically dramatized. Rather than using characters as puppets and making them serve some function of his own, whether the forwarding of the plot or the exposition of favored ideas, the writer of polyphonic fiction brings characters alive as voices, one conflicting with another. No doubt pure polyphony is beyond human reach, since no author could abnegate himself as completely as

Bakhtin's theory requires; and no doubt degrees of polyphony exist in authors other than Dostoevsky. (The irony of arguing that one and only one author really grasped the significance of human plurality was apparently missed by Bakhtin, at least at first.) Chaucer the poet possesses just the kind of telling absence called for by a theory of polyphony that has the author writing himself out of the work, as far as this is humanly possible, and surrendering it to his own creations. Just as polyphony brings together "ideas and worldviews, which in real life [are] absolutely estranged and deaf to one another, and force[s] them to quarrel,"[22] Chaucer allows a Miller to contest the worldview of a Knight—and in fact to refute it in its entirety, in the spirit of true polyphony—as would never conceivably be possible in life. But the great quarreler of the *Canterbury Tales*, and the most vocal of the pilgrims (as it happens she is half-deaf to boot), is the Wife of Bath. The Wife deals in report, not in the dignified meaning of the word but in the sense of a mix of truth, lies, rumor, and twice-told tales comparable to the old, mixed-up sense of the word "news."[23]

When in *The Merchant of Venice* word reaches Venice that Antonio's ship has wrecked, one of his friends asks whether the news is to be believed, whether "my gossip Report be an honest woman of her word." Replies his companion, "I would she were as lying a gossip as ever knapp'd [chewed] ginger or made her neighbors believe she wept for the death of a third husband."[24] The Wife of Bath feigned tears after the death of her fourth, not her third, husband, but that's a technical point. The Wife is "my gossip Report." She is gabbing, common sense, truth, and slander, all at once. Strongly associated with the world of trade,[25] she is the Venice of language where everything crosses. If seaports were cities of Babel where a multitude of languages were heard, the Wife's babble seems to contain the whole of language from biblical texts to slang. The Wife presents, indeed, a kind of living illustration of satiric excess, and in the wayward abundance of her speech is much that was later to be reduced to the straightness of philosophical and political argument.

The discourse of La Vieille in the *Romance of the Rose* is rich in satiric particularity, flooding us with specifics. The Wife's speech has the same wealth of worldly reference, the same empirical thrust, but in addition rises to the level of theory, and her espousal of an explicit theory of pluralism does much to make her the audacious figure she is. If "fourteenth-century English society may be described as unintentionally or reluctantly pluralist,"[26] the Wife's pluralism is avowed and polemical. "Everich hath of God a propre yifte, / Som this, som that, as hym liketh shifte," which makes God sound about as willful as the Wife of Bath (Wife's Prologue, ll. 103–4). "Auctoritee" itself is to the Wife of Bath one way among many. The Wife will tolerate "auctoritee" provided that it tolerate her. It was a long time before toleration was raised to philosophical repute. In Locke, certainly, the toleration argument possesses none of the flaming audacity or satiric color it does in the Prologue of the Wife of Bath. When Locke pled for the toleration of indifferent things and urged men to lay aside dubious glosses and verbal disputes in favor of plain meanings and amicable commerce, it was as if he desatirized the Wife of Bath's attack on clerical learning, her plain speaking, her commercial mentality, her contention that the decision to remarry or not is morally indifferent. And with the advent of modern civic journalism Lockean views in turn were disseminated with the help of satire so light, it is scarcely satiric.

In describing polyphony as a way of bringing into contact "ideas and worldviews, which in real life [are] absolutely estranged and deaf to one another," Bakhtin's concern is actually to distinguish the freedom of this prose mode from the tendentiousness of journalism. The tendency of Addison's journalism is to enforce the worldview of Locke, his authority on everything from the scale of Being to the nature of wit. Significantly, the persona Addison adopts is Chaucerian—that of a critical yet sympathetic, observant yet unregarded spectator and recorder.[27] In the *Spectator*, then, we seem to witness the translation of Chaucerian estates satire into journalism, much as Locke, Addison's mentor, transforms the toleration argument from satiric "game" to philosophical decency. Not only this, but Addison claims as his own the space staked out by Chaucer for fiction. The first apology for the *Canterbury Tales* might be read, in fact, as a request for the audience to indulge his fiction—indulgence being necessary because a work like the *Canterbury Tales* almost by definition doesn't fit the categories of religious and moral doctrine. While the *Tales* do contain saints' lives and moral discourses, most translate uncertainly into the language of moral statements, and in any case such exemplary material as exists in the work *is* contained, almost like speech "novelized" by incorporation into one of Bakhtin's works of prose. Chaucerian fiction opens a space independent of authority, as the tales take place literally in between that of the Knight and that of the Parson. Addison's journalistic satire claims cognizance, similarly, over human affairs outside the notice of both the law and the church. And this space, the realm of civil society, has in turn been occupied in our own day by mass media whose power is neither that of the church nor that of the state, but a third force. The tasteful miscellany of the *Spectator* yields to the modern newspaper, where "the most diverse and contradictory material is laid out, extensively, side by side and one side against the other."[28] It is as if one were reading a description of the *Canterbury Tales*.

*

The author of the *Parliament of Fowls* presents in the *Canterbury Tales* a kind of parliament of fools. It may be an accident of literary history that two of the keenest satirists in English, as unlike as they otherwise were, actually did work as parliamentary reporters (while another of the authors featured in this study wrote a series of parliamentary novels). Dr. Johnson, whose Juvenal was an austere moralist rather than the king of caricature, recorded parliamentary debates in the early 1740s, but apparently with so liberal an addition of his own genius that he quit when it became known to him that his speeches were received as authentic. He would not, he said, be "accessary to the propagation of falsehood."[29] Caught between his principles and his incapacity for mere transcription, it seems Johnson resigned his post. On his deathbed Johnson repented these productions alone among all his writings. Perhaps in something of the spirit that led Chaucer to recant such stories as the Miller's in a postscript to the *Canterbury Tales* that reads like a literary last rite, the dying Johnson "expressed his regret for his having been the author of fictions, which had passed for realities."[30] Both "reporters" made use of poetic license only to censure it in the end as the worst fabling—the one in spite of the precedent of Thucydides, the other perhaps because he was unwilling that his work of genius should *be* a precedent.

Also a parliamentary reporter was Dickens. But by the time of *Little Dorrit*, with its portrayal of parliamentary Barnacles choking the nation (and its equally satiric treatment of a public opinion beguiled with externals and awed by fraud), Dickens evidently had come to the conclusion that the demands of truth were better satisfied by satire than shorthand.[31] Throughout his work, indeed, satiric types pour forth in plenitude, as though only satire with its "fullness" were adequate to the fantastic shapes of human folly, pretense, and invention. Here too is God's plenty, all the more emphatically in that Dickens depicts social extremes that Chaucer preferred to omit, more or less, from the Canterbury pilgrimage. While the magnates of England are unrepresented on the pilgrimage and the peasants present only nominally, in the figure of a Plowman who never comes to life, Dickens doesn't shy from the portrayal of the lowest misery or the highest wealth and in fact links the two as in *Little Dorrit* itself. This technique of the strange coupling, along with his way of laying low the high and raising up the low, allies Dickens with the tradition of Menippean satire that also flows through the *Canterbury Tales*. The pilgrimage to Canterbury assembles people who would never otherwise talk so freely or even perhaps meet. But Chaucer goes only so far.

Ranging from Johnson's voice of doom to Blake's gleeful inversions of the Johnsonian wisdom to Dickens's caricatures in a spirit of excess akin to Blake's (to cite but a few of its expressions), satire itself encompasses a spectrum of moods and voices. Between Johnson and Dickens one of the traditional doctrines of poetics was shaken—that of the hierarchy of styles. When Chaucer had the Miller speak like a churl and the Knight like a noble, clearly he was maintaining the hierarchy of styles even as he allowed the Miller to unhorse the Knight. If carnival loses its meaning in the absence of moral norms whose violation is played out and whose restoration is presupposed, the *Canterbury Tales* take carnivalesque liberties without undoing the social hierarchy. The pilgrims themselves appear in roughly descending order in the General Prologue; at least the catalog begins high and ends low. Chaucer doesn't adhere to neoclassical principles, in whose light he is apt to appear gothic in the bad sense, but the incongruity of high diction and commonplace, of true and mock heroic, is as much a given to the Nun's Priest and to Chaucer himself as to Pope. Pope for his part plays with such finesse on the incongruity of the heroic and the trivial that one critic speculates Johnson wrote so little verse because he felt that after Pope poetry had nowhere to go.[32] Johnson believed in the fixity of the social hierarchy as well. There is a certain poignancy in his staunch belief in hierarchy on the very eve of the age of revolution, and in his unshakable indifference to social questions like the status of women just as they are about to explode.

A blow to the hierarchy of styles was Wordsworth's elevation of common subjects to poetic dignity (along with his espousal of an ethic of sympathy foreign to the spirit of satire). Another was the submergence of satire itself by the novel, a traditionally disreputable genre whose "rise" was such that by the age of Dickens it was capable of both social analysis and philosophical reflection. In Joyce, though, the destruction of the hierarchy of styles is perfected as impressively as Pope perfected verse satire. The very difference between true and mock heroic seems annihilated in *Ulysses*. If Leopold Bloom were no more than a counterfeit Odysseus, the traditional priority of original over copy and great over small would be left intact and *Ulysses* wouldn't be the experiment it is. And perhaps Joyce's experiment could be put this way: where Chaucer reported both the Knight's Tale, set in ancient Greece, and a subversive parody set in contemporary Oxford (with an epic span of years reduced to a few days), Joyce placed ancient and modern on the same plane, condensed years into a single day, and rehearsed a variety of voices with a fidelity that verges on absolute parody. But can Joyce be considered a "reporter" in the Chaucer tradition?

The locus classicus of the mock heroic in the *Canterbury Tales*, the Nun's Priest's Tale is something of a supertale whose debates, rhetorical devices, and thematic material parody the other tales in general. Undescribed in the General Prologue like "Chaucer" himself, the Nun's Priest thus becomes a kind of double of the poet, his wit and strategic apologies a reflection of Chaucer's own. In one disclaimer, corresponding to Chaucer's excuse for the Miller's Tale on the grounds that it belongs to someone else, the Nun's Priest alleges, "Thise been the cokkes wordes, and nat myne" (l. 3265). (Making this alibi doubly dubious is that whatever "thise" refers to is impossible to locate in the text.) The Nun's Priest, too, then, poses as a reporter of sorts. Now if *Ulysses* projects the epic past into the present moment, the Nun's Priest plunges the examples and stories of the past—things already written, prescripted—into a context where outcomes are not given in advance and life depends on the power of improvisation. If *Ulysses* is informed by the spirit of Rabelais, Rabelais in turn, we might say, magnifies to unheard-of dimensions the grandiosity, medical lore, scholastic absurdities, and rhetorical topics of the Nun's Priest's Tale. In any event Joycean parodies of things like popular romance—the Sir Thopas of his day?—bear a virtual sign reading "These are someone else's words, not mine." Not just the mixing of tongues but the placement of language itself at an ironic distance from the author—a technique that enabled the prose of the novel in the first place, in Bakhtin's view—is radicalized in *Ulysses*. A reporter strives for objectivity: Joyce at his most objective reproduces the qualities of a given tongue with an accuracy beyond the reach of journalism, capturing even shifting tones of voice. Where the reporter chronicles events, Joyce captures speech events, as with the precisely recorded inner speech of Molly Bloom, that daughter of the Wife of Bath. His too is the poet's charge: to "reherce as ny as evere he kan / Everich a word."

Joyce even referred to himself as a recorder of events. In defending the text of *Dubliners*, he wrote, "He is a very bold man who dares to alter in the presentment, still more to deform, whatever he has seen and heard. . . . I cannot alter what I have written."[33] The letter is dated from Via Giovanni Boccaccio in Trieste, and alludes to Chaucer.

CHAPTER 2

Addison: Satire and Civility

T he emergence of the modern public realm has been linked with the
coffeehouse, where newspaper readers met to discuss commerce, politics,
and culture—an institution already robust in early-eighteenth-century London.
Here for a while there flourished a journal that became a cultural event in its own
right: the *Spectator* of Addison and Steele. Widely read and admired and later
to inspire the formation of clubs and improvement societies even in Scotland
and America, the *Spectator* surveys the nation and monitors both morals and
manners, correcting faults with a gentle touch. Above all it's Addison's own
manner, at once easily decorous and lightly admonitory, that gave the *Spectator*
its magic. The modern journalist, "not as a reporter only, but as a critic,
watchdog," and voice of the public interest, is said to arrive on the public
scene in the late eighteenth century at the height of the Enlightenment.[1] The
role had already been sketched out by Addison, himself an apostle of the
philosopher of the Enlightenment, Locke.[2]

No one would maintain that freedom of speech was a thing unknown
before the coming of the coffeehouse. We need only recall the rich and
sudden outpouring of opinion during the Civil War, and the magnificent
defense of unlicensed printing it inspired in Milton, to recognize that freedom
of expression was no invention of eighteenth-century civil society. Yet the
"Areopagitica" itself burns with intolerance and actually grants the censor broad
powers, outlawing as it does not only the publication of Catholic opinion but
anything at all "which is impious or evil absolutely, either against faith or
manners."[3] That Milton himself became a licenser is not such an anomaly as
it first appears. In this context, Addison's most important contribution may
have been to spoof censorship itself by setting up as the "watchdog" of faith,
manners, and style. Simply by enacting the role so engagingly, he deprives the
censor of his awe. If Chaucer—himself renowned for the quality of tolerance—
opened space for fiction, Addison helps institute a more secular freedom of
expression.

Even as he softens and civilizes the satiric tradition and introduces a style that would pass to Austen and Trollope, Addison reminds us of Chaucer. It isn't just that the Spectator club is composed, at least in the abstract, of "such persons as are engaged in different ways of life, and deputed as it were out of the most conspicuous classes of mankind,"[4] like the Canterbury assortment; or that of these persons the good knight, Sir Roger, is introduced first, again as in Chaucer; or even that Addison's semiserious tone is a refinement of Chaucerian seriocomic. Simply as an observer of the human scene (one who possesses the same kind of social invisibility, too, as Chaucer's namesake on the pilgrimage), Mr. Spectator brings to mind Chaucer's stance as observer and reporter. Not that Addison refers to Chaucer directly. Standing in a tradition means being indirectly in touch with ancestors through others more familiar; like the strands of a web, those of tradition lead back to other strands. Addison was certainly in touch with Chaucer through Dryden, who defended, translated, and as he says venerated Chaucer as the founder of English poetry. From Dryden's tribute to Chaucer emerges the image of a writer of "wonderful facility and clearness," a "perpetual fountain of good sense" and yet modest for all that, a satirist who didn't push satire too far, an impartial and exact surveyor of "the various manners and humours (as we now call them) of the whole English nation of his age."[5] Is this not Addison's representation of himself in the *Spectator*—a man of good sense, satiric but modest, of broad views and keen vision, the impartial critic of the age? To the extent that the *Spectator*, itself wonderfully facile, contributed to the public's debate about itself,[6] this in turn was influenced by a kind of idealized image of a satirist whose greatest work *was* a debate.

Substantiating the affinity between Addison and Chaucer is that both find themselves in an increasingly market-driven society where groups share not so much a sense of the common good as a code of sociability, the sociability that is exhibited by figures like the Friar and even the Wife of Bath, and that Addison seeks to fortify with moral content. The General Prologue to the *Canterbury Tales* places us in a world fragmented into "professions," each with its own (dubious) code of practice and terms of art, their representatives distinguished by a purely social excellence. In her study of the General Prologue, Jill Mann draws a parallel between the multiplicity of "professionals" on the Canterbury pilgrimage and the division of functions in the modern city under the force of capitalism, in the process citing Louis Wirth:

> The city . . . tends to resemble a mosaic of social worlds in which the transition from one to the other is abrupt. The juxtaposition of divergent

personalities and modes of life tends to produce a relativistic perspective and a sense of toleration of difference.[7]

Addison, whose feeling for capitalism appears in his fond depiction of the Royal Exchange, is not only a voice of tolerance but a follower of Locke, philosopher of tolerance. But if the city with its fragmented life-worlds resembles a mosaic, a mosaic in turn bears a certain abstract likeness to the bits and pieces of a newspaper. Joyce may have been onto something when he took the newspaper as symbol of the capitalist order. In Addison the emergence of journalism is tied directly to the defense of commerce and the promotion of an ethos suitable in theory to the diverse character of modern life.

As readers of the *Canterbury Tales* move from the idealized past of the Knight's Tale to the Miller's Tale set in the Oxford of the present, we experience the kind of disenchantment of the world attributed by Bakhtin to the novel. Transposing the Knight's Tale into a bourgeois setting, placing it in "the zone of familiar contact" (and the jests of the tale are familiar contact all right), achieve a satiric effect.[8] When Addison attaches classical tags to familiar essays, he brings the classical ideal down to the everyday level by a kind of gentle descent, in contrast with the rude reductions of the Miller. If Addison follows Chaucer, then, it isn't Chaucer of the fabliaux—the lowest of literary forms which he elevated to high art—so much as the apologist for the fabliaux and master of ironic nuance. Throughout Chaucer and certainly in the *Canterbury Tales* the decorous and the indecorous, the polite and the crude, are bound together like mutually defining terms.[9] Addison unbinds them. Like Dryden, who left the more licentious of the *Canterbury Tales* alone for all of his love of Chaucer, Addison wants none of the crude; his affinity is with those holding up a standard of decorum or presenting an example of style for imitation (as his own model was imitated widely). By analogy with the chivalric romance that "aspires to provide norms for language in real life, to teach good style, *bon ton,* how to converse in society,"[10] Addison instructs readers unsure of the precepts of style. In turn, an Addisonian ideal of decorum informs the prose of Austen and Trollope. In this tradition concerned both with morals and manners,[11] propriety takes the form not of speeches "proper" to their several speakers so much as a binding code of conduct and style. From this perspective the more strident journalism may look like a source of rudeness, an incitement to the kind of rough-voiced controversy that is the loathing of Bakhtin's "first stylistic line." And as if in confirmation of the bond between satire and journalism, the Addisonians reduce the roughness of satire as well. In Addison's own case this means adapting satire to the rhetoric of civility and offering it in daily or journalistic doses.

From the days of the ritualized curse people have felt the importance of getting the violence of satire under control, and in Addison this project, consistent with the more general one of taming passion, takes the form of a kind of running satire on satire. Addison abstains from abusive satire, making it an object of comment instead. While prior restraint of speech ceased officially in England in 1694, the law of libel, seditious and otherwise, remained in effect. "Theoretically, one might say or print what he pleased, but he was responsible to the common law for allegedly malicious, scurrilous, scandalous, or derogatory utterances which supposedly tended toward the contempt, ridicule, hatred, scorn, or disrepute of other persons, religion, government, or morality."[12] In these circumstances Addisonian satire, with its renunciation of malice and defamation, represents not only good policy but a lesson in the difference between liberty and license; and Chaucer, understood in Dryden's sense as one who took the satire of religion only so far, is its tutelary genius. The result contributed to the building of civil society.

Of Chaucer and Addison only the latter, I imagine, hoped to disseminate a new mode of civility. Addison after all sought to influence, and did, while the very impressionability of the pilgrim Chaucer, as though he passed from one sphere of influence to another, marks him a satiric figure. If journalism today is in the business of influence, the susceptibility to that strange power makes a fool of Chaucer's namesake. In the hands of Addison influence loses its quality of the ridiculous and becomes something rational and beneficial. He practically defines what is meant by an improving influence, all the more because of his chosen role as homilist of civility. Attempting to soothe passions, promote goodwill, and divert men from the "enthusiasm" that led England to civil war not long before—a program that calls for the moderation of satire, too— Addison has a place of honor in the civilizing process that tightened the code of conduct in the modern nation-state. In retrospect the *Spectator* seems to play a part in nation building itself, diffusing norms from a strong political center and binding provinces to capital[13] as well as raising the cultural tone much as Johnson sought to do in his Dictionary (also a kind of national institution). If, as Norbert Elias, historian of the civilizing process, contends, the English forged a unique national style of civility blending a code of manners and a code of morals, nowhere is that style better or more influentially illustrated than in the *Spectator* papers of Addison.[14]

The same number of the *Spectator* in which Addison frames his policy of satiric censure also features a sort of parable of nation building. A military member of the Spectator club (we are told) objects to criticism of the army; a merchant vetoes any ridicule of "aldermen and citizens" or the bourgeoisie; a country man ridicule of country squires, "the ornaments of the English nation"; and so on. It is to resolve this tangle of conflicting interests that Addison lays down his policy of impartiality: he will reprove vice wherever it appears, but in a spirit of benevolence. He will speak without reference to persons (No. 34). Ideally, then, through the *Spectator* members of estates with their several prejudices become citizens of a nation. As commerce refines out of private interests a good beyond the intentions of the agents—a doctrine taking shape in Addison's day—so Addison, an admirer of commerce, makes a nation out of corporate interests.[15] If the civilizing effect of commerce, like the Romans but more gently and therefore more effectively, "makes human nature shine, reforms the soul, / And breaks our fierce barbarians into men,"[16] Addison imagines the transformation of social life in the image of civility— the broadening of narrow allegiances and the replacement of faction by benevolence and crudity by style.

As Elias describes it, the civilizing process promotes a more subtle observation of others and a keener sensitivity to "shades or nuances of conduct."[17] Certainly Addison promotes these things, as do novelists after him. The Spectator after all *is* an observer refining and sharpening the sensitivities of his audience. Now it is in the interest of moral progress that Addison marks the distinction between the uncouth and the polite (those contraries braided so inseparably in the gothic Chaucer). It's as if he sought to improve society at large as Horace, by checking vulgarity and uncouth usages, improved satire. If those who softened the original ferocity of Roman satire performed a civilizing act, Addison endeavors to generalize that act. And he too "wants it understood that he is a moralist, not an abuser of persons."[18] Satire as the unmasking of vice and folly involves some element of public shaming. Addison, however, administers punishment without the brute exposure of the victim to the crowd:

> If I meet with anything in city, court, or country, that shocks modesty or good manners, I shall use my utmost endeavours to make an example of it. I must however intreat every particular person who does me the honour to be a reader of this paper, never to think himself, or any one of his friends or enemies, aimed at in what is said: for I promise him, never to draw a faulty character which does not fit at least a thousand people: or to publish a single paper, that is not written in the spirit of benevolence and with a love to mankind. (No. 34)

In the spirit of the Roman law prohibiting the satirist from naming anyone living,[19] Addison lays down the law with civility. His distinction between personal and impersonal satire became conventional. Johnson codified it in his Dictionary. When Engels, having lashed the English bourgeoisie in *The Condition of the Working Class in England,* qualifies his argument in the end by noting that it is directed only at a class, not at persons, and then naming some "honourable exceptions,"[20] he makes a distinction that an ideologue might dismiss as bourgeois but another could interpret as a trace of the satiric practices underlying much modern political argument. Even Swift, whose definition of satire as "a sort of glass, wherein beholders do generally discover every body's face but their own"[21] reads like a satire of the Spectatorial policy, accepted the distinction between class and individual. Writing in the third person, Swift states, "He lashed the vice, but spared the name; / No individual could resent, / Where thousands equally were meant."[22]

While Swift's savage indignation puts him at odds with Addison, he would have agreed with the latter's aim of correcting vice and exposing folly, as well as with the general policy of tempering castigation with levity and aiming at faults rather than particular persons. In not making a public spectacle of anyone, and in staying clear of the brutality and ostentation that attend the public display of power, Addison marks the shift toward the less theatrical, more readerly realm that Habermas calls "the bourgeois public sphere." The emergence of that sphere coincides, in fact, with the creation of print-centered modes of publicity to rival the more spectacular—visual and dramatic—publicity of state power. Even so, satire calls up some feeling of the power of public rituals of justice in that, like the drama of a trial, it focuses attention on an object of judgment. Addison tempers the harshness of satire (as many a novel does the harshness of judgment) even as he calls on its power to focus a public like the drama of a trial. By holding crimes against taste up to ridicule and laying down the satiric law, he helps establish the tribunal of critical reason, the tribunal in whose name journalism still speaks. That satire retains some trace of the power of public ritual may help account for its profusion in the early years of the public realm according to the Habermasian calendar. With the opening of newly contested public space, satire strengthens claims by capturing in print some feeling, however moderated, of the ritual trial and execution of offenders.

The satirist, says Dryden, is the most delicate of hangmen. There is

a vast difference betwixt the slovenly butchering of a man, and the fineness of a stroke that separates the head from the body, and leaves it standing in its place. A man may be capable, as Jack Ketch's wife said of his servant, of a plain piece of work, a bare hanging; but to make a malefactor die sweetly was only belonging to her husband.[23]

If the civilizing process improves table manners, it also, it seems, refines hangmanship. Probably Addison wouldn't care to be likened to a Jack Ketch, even if he too is concerned with the style of his stroke. But the real irony of the use of satire as an instrument of refinement lies in the indelicacy of so much of the satiric tradition—the sheer license of the Varronian or Menippean satire, the excess of Juvenal's woman hatred, the riotous Rabelais. Even Chaucer, known for his subtlety, indirection, and courtliness, has his pilgrims lampoon one another. (Practically inciting her critics, the Wife of Bath presents a special case. Not only is she subjected to a degree of public exposure that others are spared, she embraces shame itself—embraces it with a recklessness antithetical to the poet's own ways. Dryden would translate her tale but not her prologue.) If "the qualities that morality and religion usually call ribald, obscene, subversive, lewd, and blasphemous have an essential place in literature,"[24] this is doubly true in satire. The very veils of "The Rape of the Lock" produce a voyeuristic effect. Not the least of Addison's contributions to the civilizing process, it seems, is his expurgation of satire itself. That "an abusive scurrilous style passes for satire" (No. 125) is one of his complaints against the age. Trollope, in repenting the liberties taken in his most satiric work, The Way We Live Now (a complaint against the age), confirms his membership in the tradition of Addison; toning down the heightened colors of satire in the name of civility and factual truth is like restraining license in the interest of the civilizing process.

The excesses of the seriocomic so pronounced in Swift, but not Swift alone, are tamed by Addison. A singularity of the seriocomic is that its subversive irreverence goes hand in hand with moral intention—in Rabelais, the intention implied in awakening language itself from its dogmatic slumber and stated in the letter of Gargantua to his son. In Swift it seems that obscenity and invective fuel moral argument. And in the Canterbury Tales Menippean license is placed within a moral frame of estates satire. In the fine modulation of the Addison style, in its seemingly perfect balance of gravity and levity, the paradox of the seriocomic is smoothed out. The puzzle of Socratic irony is similarly resolved.

"It was said of Socrates that he brought philosophy down from heaven, to inhabit among men; and I shall be ambitious to have it said of me, that I have brought philosophy out of closets and libraries, schools and colleges, to dwell in clubs and assemblies, at tea-tables, and in coffee-houses" (No. 10). The faint tone of the ridiculous in this analogy is fitting, for in fact Addison is so far from Socratic that he eliminates the uncertainty induced by Socratic irony—uncertainty that plays over much of the satiric tradition including the wise foolery of Chaucer. Sometimes, at the start of a paper, we don't quite know how to take Addison, or where he is going, but by the end all is revealed. Number 12 opens with an account of Mr. Spectator's strangely mute ways: "I move up and down the house and enter into all companies, with the same liberty as a cat or any other domestick animal, and am as little suspected of telling any thing that I hear or see." Momentarily we envision Addison in the role of unregarded observer held first by Lucius the ass and then the asinine Chaucer. Shortly, though, the paper turns into a sermon on the danger of ghost stories and a defense of rational religion. The uncertainty of the reader is resolved, just as the *Spectator* papers in general, by their brevity and charm, allay the anxieties of an audience new to its role as "the reading public."[25] By rationalizing the fabling and foolery of satire, Addison reassures the reader, brings forth clarity from confusion, and promotes a civilized kind of literary decorum.

And Addison deals with Chaucerian material in the same way, reducing a gothic confusion of "solaas" and "sentence" to a pleasurable course of instruction. When Addison tells a story its moral shines through every word, as is not the case with some of the most moralistic of the *Canterbury Tales* (notably the Prioress's and Physician's) or, for that matter, the Nun's Priest's Tale, which seems to mock moralization itself.[26] Chaucer's *House of Fame* is a seriocomic work calling up Ovid's temple of fame. The same temple is Addison's point of departure in Spectator No. 439 for a sermon on the meanness of spying and the nothingness of petty comments. The comic element disappears, as though Addison, not Chaucer, were following some *Ovide Moralisé*. The universe is pictured by Addison as a magnificent scale of being (one in which the kind of gaps, clashes, and anomalies that characterize the *Canterbury Tales* vanish into harmony). When in the Knight's Tale Theseus philosophizes about the "fair chain of love" that binds the universe, the reader nevertheless recalls the folly and violence of love in the tale proper, recalls too that for political reasons of his own Theseus is haranguing his sister-in-law into marriage as he once took the queen of the Amazons by force.[27] Sexual warfare in the *Spectator* is more polite. So, too, while Addison like Chaucer uses fables and dream visions, they are far more transparent, belonging as they do to a Lockean universe where words stand clearly for things. In lieu of the many-voiced fiction of the *Canterbury Tales*, Addison advances a Lockean philosophy, promotes a Lockean ideal of civility, adapts Locke's theory of instruction to the education of the public at large, and in fact cites Locke in his exposition of the scale of being.[28] As though doctrine marked the vanishing point of satire, satire in Addison disappears finally into the word of Locke. If Voltaire really believed Addison superior to Shakespeare,[29] maybe this was because only Addison received light from the very source of the Enlightenment, Locke.

A physician, Locke in turn transformed the satiric "cure" of delusion into a kind of psychomedical art, laying the foundation of the therapeutic culture we now inhabit.[30] This sort of neutralization of satire produces, it seems to me, a number of additional features of our common landscape. The "right not to understand, the right to confuse, to tease . . . , the right to not be taken literally, not 'to be oneself' "[31]—all these rights once accorded the satirist, rights that empowered Chaucer to confuse us with a foolish double of himself, condense into the right of free speech. The Rabelaisian vision of debt as the source of peace and plenty cools into Addison's idealization of Public Credit and, more generally, into the Enlightenment theory of commerce. The irreverent paradoxes of the *Fable of the Bees*—its seriocomic tone and mingled prose and verse a reminder of the Menippea—settle over time into the decency of social science. Elections, the stagiest ritual of our political life, have satiric antecedents ranging from the elevation of mock kings (a custom still alive in an English hamlet well into the eighteenth century)[32] to the choice of Harry Bailly as lord and literary critic of the Canterbury pilgrimage. There is a deep affinity between raising one up to honor in the name of the community and singling one out for dishonor and loading him with guilt and infamy, between excessive praise and excessive abuse. Addison of course is a moderate and holds his office as satirist-general by the informal consent of his readers. This in itself is a kind of lesson in Locke, just as the methods, ends, and tenor of Addisonian instruction all accord with Locke. Addison schools his readers in the norms of civil society. But even the practice of agreeing to disagree, so characteristic of modern civility, has satiric underpinnings.

In the *Parliament of Fowls* and later the *Canterbury Tales* Chaucer establishes a loose framework capable of both calling forth and containing a satiric plenitude of voices. In each work the conflicts that break out as a direct result of holiday freedom of speech are left largely unresolved and perhaps for that reason do not burst the order agreed on, or, as a Lockean might say, consented to by the parties themselves. The Canterbury company, ranging from the Knight to the Miller, and the assembly of birds from the eagles to the seed and worm eaters both represent a kind of mixed commonwealth able to accommodate a good deal of diversity.[33] Of similar but more stylish cloth is the Whig vision of a social order friendly to human variety, symbolized in the Spectator club. If Whig satire absorbs the odd one "into the club, cherishing him as a 'character,' and turning the whole cast into rather good sorts whose follies or peculiarities are largely points of view detached from actions with consequences,"[34] this in turn sounds like a prettification of the *Canterbury Tales* with its singular types and odd variety of viewpoints.

In time, as satire itself was absorbed into the novel, and as the Addisonian style of observation was adopted by Austen and Trollope, the transformation of satire initiated by Addison was taken to a new level. But "initiate" may be misleading, for just as the builders of the modern public realm took the ancients as their model, Addison in civilizing satire followed the example of Horace. It was Horace's intent to make satire elegant, to repress abuse and clowning without the appearance of constraint. And if Horace is the classical precedent for Addison's style, at once notably easy and critically attentive, he underwrites as well the conception of a text-centered public realm in which men of the pen act as the arbiters of merit and fame. Also traceable to Horace is the figure of the poet as "one who truly understands the meaning of history and individual action in a way inaccessible to the practitioners of war and politics"[35]—a figure sensed in the background behind Adam Smith's vision of actors who produce ends they never intended and Kant's belief that spectators and not the actors in the political game see things as they are,[36] and for that matter Byron's Horatian survey of the human scene in *Don Juan*, and even Trollope's renunciation of political ambition in favor of parliamentary novels and Arnold's defense of the one who removes himself from the press of practical life to see things as they are, a figure he calls the spectator.[37] In the inaugural number of the *Spectator* our narrator places himself semiseriously in this tradition:

> Thus I live in the world, rather as a spectator of mankind, than as one of the species; by which means I have made my self a speculative statesman, soldier, merchant and artizan, without ever meddling with any practical part in life. I am very well versed in the theory of an husband, or a father, and can discern the errors in the oeconomy, business, and diversion of others, better than those who are engaged in them.

Today, of course, it is the newspapers and their electronic cousins, assuming an impartiality that sets them apart from political actors, that claim the role of spectator and interpreter of the public pageant, as well as dispenser of fame. Satire has become journalism.

If Addison follows Horace, so too does Chaucer in his persona of a private, bookish man, spectator rather than actor, not a candidate for public distinction. This then is another bond between the two. In Addison's case, though, leaving fame to others was a means if not to fame itself, then at least to an influence novel in degree and kind. That effect called influence we now ascribe to the mass media—that something which has neither the force of a command nor the authority of a moral prescription but is somehow all the more insinuating for its lack of them—seems to have been practically invented by Addison. In satirizing "those vices which are too trivial for the chastisement of the law, and too fantastic for the cognizance of the pulpit" (No. 34), Addison opens space *between* law and pulpit that has since been colonized so completely by the agencies of influence, chiefly journalism.[38] When Leopold Bloom dreams of

> some one sole unique advertisement to cause passers to stop in wonders[,] a poster novelty, with all extraneous accretions excluded, reduced to its simplest and most efficient terms not exceeding the span of casual vision and congruous with the velocity of modern life,[39]

he seeks to distill the magical essence of influence, to discover the power beyond power, to bring Locke ("simplest and most efficient terms") up to the speed of modern life. By the same token, he does a kind of unwitting imitation of the first and greatest of the popularizers of Locke, Addison.[40]

Journalism of course deals in credibility, and the voice of good plain sense in which Locke writes is like the distilled essence of that quality. By aestheticizing good sense as good taste, Addison makes it that much more appealing. A countertradition makes an issue of credibility itself. From Lucian's "I humbly solicit my readers' incredulity"[41] to the confessed frauds of Chaucer's Pardoner to the not exactly incredible dream vision of *Nineteen Eighty-four*, the Menippean tradition puts a strain on the kind of belief that common sense seeks to engender. A master at turning credibility back on itself was Swift.

CHAPTER 3

Swift: The Priority of Satire

Addison is a philosophical son of Locke, citing him in the *Spectator*, taking the same view of the ends of government, and displaying as a preceptor of morals and manners the "humane, friendly, civil temper" Locke's theory of education calls for in a tutor.[1] The influence of Locke owes something to the qualities of goodwill and civility informing his own writings—the evoked presence of a humane and reasonable man—as well as to his skill in grounding scientific knowledge. Science and humanitarian benevolence remain to this day the twin pillars of the dominant system of values, a system epitomized in the figure of the medical researcher or, for that matter, the social scientist, laboring for the good of humanity. Exactly the figure of the humane and reasonable man of facts is showcased in what is probably the best-known piece of satiric writing in English: Swift's "A Modest Proposal." The extreme dimness of this humanitarian places him, however, in the tradition of the modest narrator of the General Prologue of the *Canterbury Tales*, whose descriptions are also in many cases a miracle of blindness.

Underlying such kinship as exists between Swift and Chaucer—both masters of indirection, but one given to a kind of Socratic humility, the other to molten hatred—is their use of the Lucianic persona, with Swift employing masks to great effect and Chaucer presenting himself in the figure of a nonentity. Where the gullible Chaucer seems to pass from the orbit and influence of one fellow traveler to another (among them a lawyer and a physician, pet Swiftian targets), Gulliver ends up assimilating himself to the horses he so admires. Where the portraits of the pilgrims seduce us momentarily into uncritical assent, so that we find ourselves applauding the Friar for his corruption and the Shipman for his ruthlessness, Swift lures us with the appearance of rationality until we find ourselves assenting to the monstrous, such as the modest proposal. Even a difference is instructive.

The fur lining of the Monk's sleeve, the ornamental silver of the Guildsmen's knives, the headgear of the Wife of Bath—the pilgrim Chaucer is taken

45

with any sort of imposing or alluring appearance. All such visual niceties are missing in "A Modest Proposal," as though the piece marked the passage into the realm of "critical reason." The narrator of "A Modest Proposal" is taken with numbers. If the pilgrim is saved from questioning his judgments by a kind of implicit sense of being an average man, the proposer deals in good rough numerical averages. In effect Swift has translated the impercipience of the pilgrim Chaucer into the terms of modern reason, and the journalistic fiction of the *Canterbury Tales* into something closer to journalism as we know it.

"A Modest Proposal," of course, offers a mock solution to the misery entailed on Ireland by the overpopulation of its poor on the one hand and the exactions of the English on the other. Our narrator, a rational-seeming man with a head for figures, concludes that in these circumstances the only hope for Ireland lies in butchering human yearlings for sale to the wealthy, thus converting the liability of starving children into an economic asset.

> Whereas the maintenance of an hundred thousand children, from two years old, and upwards, cannot be computed at less than ten shillings a piece per annum, the nation's stock will be thereby encreased fifty thousand pounds per annum, besides the profit of a new dish, introduced to the tables of all gentlemen of fortune in the kingdom, who have any refinement in taste.[2]

If Ireland has been reduced to such misery that selling human flesh for cash looks like a way out, blame must go to the English as well as those wealthier citizens of Ireland itself who connive in the oppression of their nation. But if these are the objects of Swift's indignation, the focus of his ridicule seems to be a certain reform mentality, a mentality strangely like the one behind the reform of the Poor Law in 1834. Inspired by the reasonings of one who asked whether an average child was worth more or less than nothing, and calculated to make the workhouse so intolerable that the poor would choose anything else in preference, the New Poor Law had in its beneficence, as one commentator has said, "a touch of insanity."[3] Yet Swift's satire continues to apply even now, long after the workhouse has receded from memory. While no one today is going to propose dressing infant skin for leather, every one of us is habituated to the same language of problem solving, the same appeal to words like "cheap, easy, and effectual," the same show of humane concern and the same statistical displays as in "A Modest Proposal." It has all become the evening news. Turn on the news and someone wearing an expression of benevolence informs you whether an index is going up or down and how imports stand to exports, before glancing, perhaps, at the issues of abortion, homelessness, and poor relief at the heart of "A Modest Proposal." Swift's abhorrence has become our norm. Satire has become journalism; or rather, the object of Swift's satire has become our journalist. The weird accuracy of Swift's depiction of the reasonable man, in spite of its strokes of exaggeration and flourishes of the fantastic, reminds us of satire's power to capture truth.

Just as Book IV of *Gulliver's Travels* leaves us unable to live with humankind even though we have no option to abandon it, "A Modest Proposal" leaves us filled with abhorrence yet unable to say for certain whether such a scheme would be more barbaric than none at all.[4] Rather than supplying us with a position, Swift deprives us of one—leaves us nowhere to stand. How then could "A Modest Proposal" be squared with any generic political position?

Withering in its caricature of a scheme for reform, "A Modest Proposal" might be read as an expression of conservatism, with the narrator possessing the classic traits of the do-gooder as seen through conservative eyes, such as shallowness of brain and a way of getting lost in the vapors of his own schemes. In advocating the eating of human flesh (it might be said), the projector simply proves his complete estrangement from the norms of common usage to which conservatism appeals. Yet "A Modest Proposal" does not reduce to a conservative polemic. A conservative polemic would have conveyed the feeling that the poor are always with us and nothing is to be done about their plight beyond the usual charity, rather than a boiling indignation at the indifference on all sides to the Irish poor and in fact a reiteration of the author's own proposals for their relief. Anyway, not until the age of the French Revolution did conservatism come into its own. Burke's portrayal of the race of "sophisters, economists, and calculators" does have something in it of Swiftian abhorrence, yet the author of "A Modest Proposal" does not take the matter of modesty so solemnly that like Burke he beautifies "all the decent drapery of life" as a chivalric grace.[5] For what it may be worth, the narrow and doctrinaire spirit of Burke's views on poor relief in his "Thoughts and Details on Scarcity" is also far from the liberal anger of "A Modest Proposal." Matthew Arnold was certainly a conservative—contemplating the same set of issues from a point of view opposed to J. S. Mill's—but in taking his catchphrase "sweetness and light" from Swift, he is careful to note the satirist's deficiency of sweetness. (In Arnold himself satire declines to a kind of petulant sarcasm.) Just as that "eminent French physician" Rabelais seems out of place in a conservative paper, Swift's eccentric fury and unconventional warfare in and of themselves violate the decorum that a more truly conservative temper would observe. An astute reader of Swift notes "how radical a position was being taken," at the end of the war between the ancients and the moderns, "by the most conservative man ever engaged on either side."[6] If the conservative defends established institutions from a position firmly within them, the oddity of Swiftian satire, in addition to its notable lack of decorum, is its sheer violence, more suggestive of attack than defense in the first place.[7]

So imprecisely does "A Modest Proposal" match conservative specifications that it could just as well be read as an example of the dismantling of an opponent's very mentality that came to be a favored tactic of the radical left. Such argument is marked not only by a general tone of scorn and ridicule clearly of satiric origin, but by a kind of dissection of the head of the foe, a laying bare of the way it forms its schemes. In his self-delusion the enemy presents a picture of "false consciousness . . . a totally distorted mind which falsifies everything which comes within its range."[8] "A Modest Proposal" is a study from within of a totally distorted mind, one that proves how warped it is when it imagines itself exhibiting the most admirable benevolence. (In this respect everything the proposer says is self-defeating. To show the other as working against himself, "planting the seeds of his own destruction," is another key tactic of modern polemic.) Thus we meet an archetype of the argument that takes apart not so much the claims of an opponent as the brain that conceives them, a practice that hardened into the political psychiatry for which the Soviet Union became infamous. Strip "A Modest Proposal" of its art and it becomes straight political analysis of error. With its transformation into ideology, which is to say a closed system, satire loses its outstanding quality, freedom.[9] Speech itself goes rigid, becoming one great repetition. How much is lost in this mechanization of satiric insight is suggested by the name of Swift, together with his predecessors Chaucer, Rabelais, Cervantes—whose Quixote too is capable of falsifying everything that comes within his range.[10]

Swift does not conform to our categories. In a sense, he doesn't even conform to his own categories. If the noble Houyhnhnms of *Gulliver's Travels* are his ideal, how much of their immunity to passion did Swift, a poet of indignation and ridicule, possess? Where Swift most clearly divides from the Houyhnhnms is in the audacity of his fictions. Such Spartans are the Houyhnhnms that they have no literature, no term for "lie" or even "opinion," and (we have to conclude) no conception, let alone tolerance, of inventions like Swift's own. Amid such starvation of the word, such absolute hostility to the freedom in which he delighted, Swift would not have lasted a day.

*

A quarter century before "A Modest Proposal" Swift impersonated a Grub Street Hack who uses some of the same accents of humble common sense, in spite of the same pretense of being a boon to humanity, as the maker of the proposal. If the proposal reads like something hatched in a garret by a mind out of touch with the real, the Hack lives in a garret in fact. Swift's partiality for the ancients and contempt for the vanity of moderns like the Hack make him a natural antagonist of journalism if only because of its recency. As opposed to the endurance of the satiric tradition, journalism seems a fashion of the moment, the word itself suggesting something short-lived, of a day. The pride swelling the author of some pamphlet destined for immediate oblivion is both grotesque and galling to Swift. (Leopold Bloom's use of newspaper in the jakes is a Swiftian touch, Swift himself having marked down the jakes as one of the destinations for the printed ephemera of his day.)[11] And there is still an element of pertinence to his perception, for if journalism boasts of being up to the minute, by the same token it perishes with the moment.

In Swift it is as though journalism were subjected to the power of the satiric tradition from which it descends in the first place, a poetically just fate for a modern.[12] The merchant, notes Defoe, dispatches his ships from port to port with the aid of a "strange and universal intelligence," in other words news;[13] Swift in "A Modest Proposal" converts the strange and the universal into the weird and the anonymous. If Defoe himself is a type of the journalist, significantly he also exemplifies a lot of what Swift detests—nonconformity, a projector's mentality, economic activism, and a protean quality, a way of shifting from one thing to another like the clouds in the Preface to *A Tale of a Tub* that look like an ass's head one minute, only to dissipate the next. The clouds, reminders of Aristophanes, are fitting symbols of the fumes and vanities of modernism from Swift's point of view. For Swift the moderns are distinguished by an absurd insolence, a disregard of things given and established; hence the necessity of satire. *Robinson Crusoe* is corrected with *Gulliver's Travels.*[14] Journalism, a modern, is corrected with satire, an ancient.

In reading Swift, we are introduced, in any event, to a tradition of satiric liberty antedating what we know now as journalism. Rekindled in *Gulliver's Travels* is some original sense of "report" itself as a "carrying back" of tales from across the sea, not so much as in *Robinson Crusoe* as in Lucian's "True History" or, in a precedent cited by Lucian and recast by Joyce, Odysseus' narration to the court of Alcinous. Report in Lucian's sense is a play on human credulity, in Swift's a kind of crafty seduction of belief; and while Lucian is a truthful enough historian to declare his own lies, in the hands of Swift credibility itself verges on the unbelievable. The Hack doesn't sustain our belief so much as raise it up again and again out of its own ashes. "Last week I saw a woman flayed, and you will hardly believe how much it altered her person for the worse."[15] For a moment, and only that, the statement conveys the impression of an authentic account.

But what is it that authenticates the "I," the Hack himself? The answer can only be his resemblance to other hacks, that is, his lack of the very originality that he like all of his kind must claim. In distinguishing himself from the multitude of writers—"whereof the whole multitude of writers most reasonably complains"[16]—the Hack simply proves himself one of them. (The same contradiction is explored more radically, but still from within, in the Underground Man whose "most 'personal' longings are only commonplace quotations from Rousseau, Byron, Pushkin, Lermontov, etc., etc.,"[17] as though he himself had become one of those literary scrapbooks that figure in *A Tale of a Tub*. The Underground Man craves but is denied the taste of novelty, originality, independence.) By now, however, the contradictions of the Grub Street Hack have been thoroughly institutionalized. Even in proclaiming a new order of things, a world so modern that Swift himself has become an ancient, our press repeats things more copiously than the worst of the Grub Street borrowers. Repeating the appropriate formulas with a show of delivering something entirely new—the news itself—makes for credibility.

Swift is a master but not the inventor of the credibility effect. The credibility effect seems a way of drawing the reader into a fiction that might otherwise be written off as fantastic.[18] Its roots go down into the satiric tradition at least as far as the "completely credible" yet outrageously satiric narration of "The Widow of Ephesus" in the *Satyricon* of Petronius.[19] In the case of Swift credibility comes of letting some fictitious other speak in character—the suppression of editorial comment being another bequest from satire to journalism. Swift loves to suppress his own judgment, achieving by the appearance of mere report effects that could hardly be attained by the figures of rhetoric. (It is hard to see how techniques as odd as the negation of one's own voice and the minimization of description, both now associated with journalism, could have originated but for the sake of some unusual effect.) The Swiftian technique of "apparent objectivity" passed to others, too, notably Smollett, where it produces scathing portraiture in the very diction of Augustan decorum; and from Smollett to Dickens.[20] Hence the prominence of Dickens in Bakhtin's discussion of the art of "pseudo-objectivity" in *The Dialogic Imagination*. And perhaps we might read the supreme objectivity of the last episode of *Ulysses*— that is, the erasure of any sign of authorial presence, let alone commentary— as a kind of transcending completion of this tradition of report, by analogy with treatment in *Ulysses* of the device of the mock heroic from Swift's era. Anyway, silencing one's own voice is tantamount to letting other voices speak, as Chaucer does in the *Canterbury Tales*. The most striking of those voices—it leaps from the page, and within the fiction itself provokes a reply from one pilgrim after another—belongs to a merry widow in the Petronian tradition, the Wife of Bath.[21]

The quality of voice answering voice that so distinguishes the *Canterbury Tales* is also present in Rabelais. In the middle of "A Modest Proposal" we are told on the authority of this eminent physician that owing to the virtues of a fish diet an increase in births takes place nine months after Lent (increase itself being the master trope of Rabelaisian rhetoric). Now if the physician Locke underwrites the moderns, from a satiric point of view Rabelais stands as both precedent and corrective of Locke, precedent in that he too anatomizes, inquires, clears away mystification, rejects the apparatus of scholasticism; corrective if only in that *Gargantua and Pantagruel* is rich in dialogue, while Locke's *Essay* centers on the workings of the single mind. The image of the single mind at work reappears in Swift as the spider of the "Battle of the Books," as well as the Grub Street Hack and the modest proposer, both of them busy solitaries lost in their own imaginings. The dialectical aspect of Rabelais, for its part, reappears in the question-answer scenes of *Gulliver's Travels*, as between the hero and the king of the giants—those Gargantuans. It seems to me that Rabelais also poses both a precedent for and a satire on modern economic thinking. If Swift reminds moderns of dialectic and restores credibility—the credit of the modern information economy—to a satiric function, through Rabelais he is in touch with the satiric predecessor of economic modernism.

In the great barrel of *Gargantua and Pantagruel* is a paean to debt as the bond that holds things together, guarantor of human amity:

> Imagine to yourself [a] world in which everyone lends and everyone owes, where all are debtors and all are lenders. Oh, what a harmony there will be in the regular motions of the heavens! I believe that I can hear them just as clearly as Plato did. What sympathy there will be between the elements! Oh, how Nature will delight in her works and productions! Ceres will be loaded with corn; Bacchus with wines. . . . Among mankind peace, love, affection, fidelity, repose, banquets, joy, gladness, gold, silver, small change, chains, rings, and merchandise will pass from hand to hand. No lawsuits, no war, no strife.[22]

Here in the shape of satire, it seems to me, is the germ of the Enlightenment theory of commerce as a civilizing force and promoter of human affections, transforming rough passion into civil sentiment.[23] (The standard metaphor of the circulation of wealth picks up the discourse on the circulation of the blood in the speech just cited—all the body's organs being at once creditor and debtor.) Among the exponents of the new theory of commerce is Addison, in whom the Rabelaisian vision of gladness becomes a vision of the Royal Exchange and the felicity of commerce. With his way of making us believe the impossible, it is as though Swift were satirizing the very process of investing belief that is idealized in Addison's allegory of Public Credit. What is seriocomic in Rabelais has begun to settle into an article of economic faith in Addison. In turn, it is from the Enlightenment study of the "regular motion," as well as the modes of "sympathy," introduced by commerce into human affairs that the social sciences took their rise.[24] Seeing that the language of social science is now popularized by the press, it appears Addison pointed the direction of modern journalism in propagating the theory of commerce as a civilizing influence.

By today Rabelais's flights of economic thought have long since settled into the regular motions of social science, just as the weird benevolence of "A Modest Proposal" has settled into the ethos of rational journalism. And if reading Swift enables us to see journalism as a kind of deadened satire, this is also true, as it happens, of Rabelais, for the barrel of *Gargantua and Pantagruel* also contains a lot of the things that now fill the news—health advice, debates, sayings and doings of the larger-than-life, even facts and figures:

> Then, with a smile, he undid his magnificent codpiece and, bringing out his john-thomas, pissed on them so fiercely that he drowned two hundred and sixty thousand, four hundred and eighteen persons, not counting the women and small children.[25]

(An act recalled when Gulliver douses the Lilliputian fire "in three minutes.") In this Bakhtin sees a parody of "dry accounts of natural disasters."[26] Disaster remains a journalistic genre to this hour, the conversion of bad news into good stories showing that Swift's ironies aren't so fantastic after all. The dry language of "A Modest Proposal" is something like the vinous language of Rabelais in reverse.

*

A favorite device of Swift is the use of average-seeming figures—a Gulliver midway between the Yahoos and the Houyhnhnms (or, for that matter, greater than the Lilliputians, smaller than the giants), a projector who both vaunts and effaces himself and proposes something at once barbaric and benevolent. Ronald Paulson calls this figure the middleman, an apt term inasmuch as he also represents a sort of merchant of generic ideas. The Swiftian intermediate has since grown into the "media."[27]

An accomplished popularizer, as we know, was Addison, his style a perfect mean between gravity and levity. With the declared intent of bringing philosophy "out of closets and libraries, schools and colleges, to dwell in clubs and assemblies, at tea-tables, and in coffee-houses" (whereas Swift liked to keep the few and the many distinct), Addison introduced the reading public to the thought of Newton and especially Locke.[28] A kind of philosophical warrant for his role as an intermediary of ideas was afforded by Locke's own conception of the scale of Being as a perfect continuum, an orderly series with every "middle space" well occupied.[29] By means of his popularizations Addison does homage not only to Locke but also, in a way, to the Creator who disseminates the gift of Being through the entire expanse of a richly populated universe. (The idea that the plenitude of beings exhibits the bounty of God—could this underwrite the "law" that population is the riches of a nation, which somehow fails to hold true of Ireland?)

An heir of the Enlightenment, and also an adept popularizer of ideas, was Freud's nephew Edward Bernays, inventor of public relations as we know it.[30] By putting to use the movers of the public mind, whether health commissioners or the authorities of fashion, Bernays was able to sway opinion in his clients' favor, but always with an aspect of promoting "the public good of my country, by advancing our trade, . . . relieving the poor, and giving some pleasure to the rich," in the words of the modest proposer. Among his favorite devices was placing "news" in the press, gaining the civic authority of print for his schemes. Perhaps the most curious of middlemen, though, is Leopold Bloom, the fictional cousin of Bernays[31] who acts as a commercial go-between and in the Bag of Wind episode tries to arrange a puff for his client Keyes. In the rattling machinery of "Aeolus" the figures of machine and wind that preside over the Swiftian world, symbols respectively of crazy schemes and the exaltation of self, come into perfect alignment; but in Bloom the abstract benevolence of the Swiftian author gives way to the felt compassion of a man of flesh. Just as Molly Bloom is too embodied to be a mere figment of the antifeminist tradition, so (I'll argue) Leopold Bloom transcends the satiric figures that underlie him. Yet if Gulliver himself goes from a generic figure to a human being in the course of his story, as some believe—at the very least he proves impossible to type as a mere Yahoo—then in a sense Bloom's humanity fulfills the tradition of Swift rather than just departing from it, a supreme example of the quickening of satiric figures that begins for our purposes with Chaucer.[32]

CHAPTER 4

Interlude: Satire and Modern Political Argument

S atire likes to strip the mask of appearance to expose a hidden truth. In the romantic movement that rose in response to the French Revolution and its cult of transparency, the symbol is valued precisely for the mystery of its revelation. Perhaps the romantic discovery of the symbol in all its translucency contributed to satire's fall from the poetic eminence it had as recently as the time of Johnson. Certainly there is little of the salt of satire in Wordsworth (who envisions a world consecrated by an invisible power), while the most satiric of his English contemporaries, Byron, some hesitate to class as a romantic at all. Yet satire was also upstaged by events outside the domain of literature, especially some of the more direct political after-effects of the French Revolution.

In Swift the satiric attitudes of indignation and disgust are expressed with such force and even relish that they resist the author's effort to moralize them. Johnson in his funereal satire on "The Vanity of Human Wishes" moralizes scorn and disgust by elevating them into a general contemptus mundi (as he converts satiric excess into a heavily redundant litany of dismal examples). A more uncontroversial admonition than "Think not the doom of man reversed for thee" is hard to imagine. We all die. Whether or not Johnson felt that after Pope poetry had nowhere to go,[1] "The Vanity of Human Wishes" does land us in a kind of dead end. But it was the appropriation of what I have called its excess potential by political doctrines in the age of revolution, on whose eve Johnson died, that really threatened the satiric tradition with closure. The futility of human ambitions would itself be codified as political doctrine, becoming what Albert O. Hirschman in his survey of conservative arguments calls the futility thesis. The futility thesis is a sharp way of stating that, politically speaking, the more things change, the more they remain the same. Often phrased with a kind of insulting wit, futility arguments "deride or deny efforts at, and possibilities of, change, while underlining and perhaps celebrating the resilience of the status quo."[2] They amount, in other words, to pronouncements of doom on given political projects. It's as though Johnson's comprehensive satire had shrunk to the level of debating tactics, and his sonority to sounding rhetoric, at the same time that his rather axiomatic argument gave way to assertions with the sound of final truths, even "laws," like "the more things change, the more they remain the same." Such exploitation of satire is characteristic of modern political doctrine generally.

As Gordon Wood has argued, the enlightened of eighteenth-century Europe and America were much given to conspiracy thinking, ascribing events to the sinister intentions of their presumed designers just as you might trace an effect to a cause. Beneath the mask of rectitude worn by actors on the political stage lay malice. The eighteenth century also, Wood notes, favored satire, the literary mode that most delights in unmasking. Between satire and conspiracy thinking Wood posits something like the one-to-one correspondence that the suspicious themselves established between effects and causes, events and intentions, outcomes and designs. As one might say, Wood finds it no coincidence that satire flourished in an age of suspicion. "Satire was made for an enlightened age."[3] Yet satire both precedes and outlives the Enlightenment. To me it seems that those possessed by the vision of cloaked intentions—a "paranoia" that reached its highest pitch during the French Revolution—reduced the serious play and allowed liberties of satire to the simplicity of a catchword, impoverishing the very source they tapped. Such usage of satire, again, characterizes a lot of the argument that flows from the age of Enlightenment.

Driven to the exposure of hypocrisy, satire portrays a world in which attempts to mask folly and corruption only illustrate the things they are supposed to hide. Stupidity

> strives in spite of nature to create Progress yet always produces its opposite. The rise becomes a fall, the advance a circular wandering, the brave new world a living hell; the search for the philosophers' stone eats up the wealth it was intended to produce; the dunce who sets up for a wit only succeeds in making his weakness apparent.[4]

With the coming of the French Revolution and its turn to terror, statism, and war, the traditional satiric insight into the vain, self-defeating effort "to create Progress" was converted into the founding principle of conservatism (which must have derived persuasive power from its deep literary resonance). As Hirschman has shown, modern conservatism originates in a conviction of the perversity of the pursuit of progress—perverse because bound to generate the opposite result—inspired by the catastrophe of the French Revolution.

> It is not just asserted that a movement or a policy will fall short of its goal or will occasion unexpected costs or negative side effects: rather, so the argument goes, *the attempt to push society in a certain direction will result in its moving all right, but in the opposite direction. . . .* Attempts to reach for liberty will make society sink into slavery, the quest for democracy will produce oligarchy and tyranny. . . . *Everything backfires.*[5]

The wealth, the excess, of the satiric tradition is thus reduced to a single flat, and now entirely dubious, proposition. In fact the traditional satiric feeling for the authority of experience—the sense that "experience is bigger than any set of beliefs about it"[6]—was itself reduced in conservatism to the doctrine that the experience of past ages is superior to the abstract schemes of reason. No doubt Swift so believed, too, but who could square the excessive indignation and disgust in *Gulliver's Travels*, indeed its indictment of standing institutions and its final troubled dream of utopia, with a set of conservative theses? The reduction of the vision of human self-defeat to conservatism entails the same kind of loss—satiric excess now being tied up in doctrine, and criticism of theory now become a theory.

Conservative formulations of the perversity and futility principles draw strength from the traditional belief that the nature of things is static and unalterable. All the more significant, therefore, is Adam Smith's argument that attempts to dam the course of economic progress prove foolish and injurious. Now it is change itself that takes on something of the character of a law not to be cheated. Nevertheless, as his moments of sardonic eloquence convince us, Smith is still in touch with the satiric tradition, and if his thought looks "either liberal or conservative, depending on which aspects are turned towards us,"[7] one reason may be its bond with a tradition deeper and older than either school. In Smith's belief that we do best to attend to our own concerns, no matter if their remoter implications escape us, there is even a reminder of the Lucianic ethos that it is better to live the common life than theorize about first and final causes.

At any rate, it's not only conservatism that conscripts satire for its own ends, any more than conservatives are the only ones to use the rhetorical devices cataloged by Hirschman.[8] Both left and right, and particularly perhaps the former, have been drawn to satire as a way of taking the war to the very citadel of the enemy, his mind. Don Quixote is in the grip of a mania interfering with his perception of the real world (as is the Hack of Swift's *Tale of a Tub* in his own way).[9] Both the Marxist and the conservative users of perversity arguments portray the objects of their enmity as lying similarly under a delusion that blocks their apprehension of a great and simple fact, the fact that reality itself stands in the way of their ideas. The mind laid bare in all its pitiful delusion is thus Quixotic, without the saving grace that Don Quixote himself possesses in such abundance. With its penchant for political psychiatry, the left, as I've said, is especially given to the diagnosis of mental errors, a practice taken so far in the former Soviet Union that criticism of the official line could be construed as an "obsession from which the patient must be cured."[10] To expose and correct mental errors is an aim at least as old as the *Consolation of Philosophy*, a classic of Menippean satire; the novelty of the Soviet practice lay in the ruthless transcription of the cure *into* practice.

Clearly, then, conservatism is not alone in laying claim to satire's power. If satire strips away disguise, demystifiers of the aristocratic regime in the eighteenth century elevated "transparency" to a political principle and exposed artifice with a kind of satiric effect. Throughout the century mock elections were held at the hamlet of Garrat near London, with the deformed and the disreputable assuming the title of mayor. Radical critics of the existing order worked to transform these wine-drenched proceedings into a simple, even transparent morality play exposing the corruption of government. A burlesque charged with the most ambiguous satiric potential was thus converted "into a radical sign for the times."[11] The construction of radical signs was also part of the agenda of the French Revolution. Heroic images of the people were fashioned that were meant to be entirely transparent and self-interpreting, images "coming close to the zero-point of representation, in which there is no metaphorical content."[12] The violence of satire, its drive to purge and punish, was itself rendered literal in the Revolution. If satire exposes hypocrisy, the unmasking of hypocrites became the obsession of the French Revolution in its most radical phase, the phase that provided the most vivid illustration of the conservative thesis that grabbing at liberty produces only despotism. And the mania for "publicity," as it was called, was fueled by a journalism that in turn claimed the satiric prerogative of exposure. The *libelles* of the 1780s that brewed the radical ideology of the French Revolution were like political fabliaux, scurrilous, anecdotal, stereotyped, the inside view of a world of cuckolds and lechers.[13] The hunt for hypocrites in any event represents a deadly ritualization of satiric practice; the penetration of disguise in which satire delights is converted to an instrument of terror.

Nor was a kind of programmatic hatred of artifice and hypocrisy confined to the Revolution. At war with these evils, but repelled by the excesses of the

Revolution and more intent on checking power than unleashing it, Jeremy Bentham too was inspired by a will to transparency. Hence, for example, his famous design for a prison that would leave inmates nowhere to hide from the inspector's eye. Intended as a "model community subject to the dictates of reason alone,"[14] the Panopticon reads like some French Revolution under a glass dome. As though rationalizing the action of satire, Bentham envisions a world with mystery and illusion stripped away. Recall that Johnson's satire on "The Vanity of Human Wishes" opens, "Let Observation, with extensive view, / Survey mankind, from China to Peru." In describing his sensation on reading Bentham's exposition of the happiness principle, John Stuart Mill records that he "felt taken up to an eminence from which I could survey a vast mental domain," a height that conferred "superiority to illusion,"[15] as if supreme clarity of vision belonged not to Johnson, resigned to the frustration of human wishes, but to the active promoter of happiness itself. Exposing other modes of reasoning as so much imposture, Bentham's thought acts with the force of satire, a force now all the more effective because arrayed in so rational a form.

The attempt to engineer progress is bound to yield a perverse result, according to the conservative. But what of the Marxist claim that all of the advances brought about by the bourgeoisie, all of its industrial power, all of its disturbance of traditional relations, will in the end only make for the ruin of the bourgeoisie itself? Evidently Marxism has its own store of perversity arguments—arguments that represent a kind of petrified satire. When Engels declares love of money the "ruling passion" of bourgeois life, he uses traditional satiric psychology; in defending acts of violence on the part of the working classes for "tearing off [the] mask of hypocrisy, so as to reveal the true state of affairs," he reduces the action of satire to warfare.[16] Marx himself had a strong satiric streak, pausing, for example, in his statement of the Communist position to comment on the great pleasure "our bourgeois" take "in seducing each other's wives."[17]

Satire is filled with actions that rebound on the actor as if to illustrate some perversity effect: the trickster tricked. In the *Canterbury Tales* the rebound principle seems to inform the debate generally, with the words of speakers coming back to haunt them in the mouths of others. A special application of the principle is given by the Wife of Bath, that voice for the authority of experience, whose strategy is to throw men's words back at them.[18] And the polemical accent of the Wife's manifesto is something like that of the most famous manifesto of all, with the difference that her performance is seriocomic and Marx's in deadly earnest. Listen to Marx disputing his opponents, quoting their own terms and tenets back to them in mockery, and you hear the note of the Wife of Bath, but without the quality Chaucer calls "game" that ambiguates everything she says. Declaring her views for all to hear and with a maximum of scandal, mocking her opponents and impersonating their voices (and reducing marriage to a cash connection), the old Wife brings to life the bourgeoisie in the hour of its youth. Where the Wife overturns "auctoritee" in the name of her own audaciously commercial ethos, Marx overturns the bourgeois order itself. Her somersaults, his tactic of satiric inversion. ("In bourgeois society capital is independent and has individuality, while the living person is dependent and has no individuality.")[19] But in spite of its undercurrent of satiric sport, there is a fundamentalist quality in the *Communist Manifesto*. Satire has hardened into system, a single quarreling voice into the last word of human history. Persuaded that capitalism contains the seeds of its own destruction, Joyce at one point in the first draft of his *Portrait of the Artist* takes the tone of the *Communist Manifesto*.[20] Later, in effect returning to the springs, he re-creates the Wife of Bath in Molly Bloom.

Different interests, anyway, exploit the rich ore of satire for their own uses. Among the standard arguments of conservatism, closely allied in fact with its doctrine of perversity, is the claim that a given measure is doomed to fail; if it will not backfire, at least it's destined to come to nothing. Once again the satiric ring of this jeer must have enhanced its rhetorical effect. Yet the futility card has been played by the left as well; what else is the assertion that resisting the overthrow of capitalism is useless, since its fall is decreed by the laws of history—an argument that more than any other, perhaps, accounts for the power of Marxist rhetoric? Nor were the Marxists the first to employ "progressive" variants of the futility thesis. Byron in *Don Juan* portrays the agents of repression, not from China to Peru but across the breadth of Europe, as a sort of brotherhood of the vain, engaged in a pursuit as blind as the denial of death. Perversity claims are made, too, as when schemes and ambitions are fulfilled in reverse. (In the first canto alone, Don Alfonso, in trying to save his honor, makes himself a figure of ridicule, and Donna Inez, intending to mend her son's morals, launches him out of her control entirely.) I want to say, though, that even while making his political case, Byron goes back to the satiric origins of arguments like the perversity thesis, seeking the freedom lost with the hardening of satire into political creed and indulging a license so free that his seriocomic performance mocks even itself. If the most extreme rhetoric of the French Revolution was forged in the *libelles* of the 1780s with their fabliaulike exposés of lechery and impotence, the first canto of *Don Juan* features a pure fabliau with a May–December marriage at its center; and so far from writing with the fanatic political moralism of the libelist the poet makes his innocent hero not only an aristocrat but one whose name connotes the ultimate libertinism. Rather than reiterate the radical line, Byron in this "ever varying rhyme" returns to its sources in a satiric tradition whose license defies reduction to a line at all.[21]

Byron's choice of a roving aristocrat as a hero also puts him in direct opposition to Wordsworth, the partisan of humble and rustic life. In an originally unprinted preface, in fact, Byron spars with the poet even before introducing his hero. Instead of making sense, Wordsworth just drivels, as though his quest for the simplicity of Nature resulted only in dullness (the perversity thesis as literary criticism).

> The pond [in "The Thorn"] is described according to mensuration: 'I measured it from side to side, 'Tis three feet long and two feet wide.' Let me be excused from being particular in the detail of such things, as this is the sort of writing which has superseded and degraded Pope in the eyes of the discerning British public, and this man is the kind of poet who, in the same manner that Joanna Southcote found many thousand people to take her dropsy for God Almighty re-impregnated, has found some hundreds of people to misbelieve his insanities. . . . [Wordsworth] would reduce [his visions] into a system of prosaic raving, that is to supersede all that hitherto by the best and wisest of our fathers has been deemed poetry—

both "system" and offenses against language being traditional prey of satire. It is satirically just, however unjust otherwise, that a poet who spoke of the press as an agency of depravity should have been lampooned in a work strewn with topical references, such as that to Joanna Southcote. "Prosaic," too, may be a cut at Wordsworth's theory that poetry is really but metrical prose. And in another stroke of mock justice, the critic of rhyme is ridiculed in a poem embellished with the most flamboyant and indeed self-satirizing rhymes in English literature. Especially striking, though, is the reference to Pope as one of "the best and wisest of our fathers" by the noted libertine and outrager of conservative opinion, and this not only because Pope framed the standard of Dullness by which Wordsworth is being convicted, and perfected the heroic couplet cast by Wordsworth into oblivion. Why should Byron have cited Pope at all if his intent was to polemicize for the liberal cause and remind his opponents of the futility of their position? How much of a liberal was Pope? For that matter, what kind of enemy of the patriarchal order cites "the best and wisest of our fathers" in a spirit of reverence? Byron's aim in *Don Juan*—a work whose satiric form, if that is the word, allows him to say virtually anything at any time—seems less to enforce a political thesis than to revive the spirit of satire in which perversity and futility arguments originate and take the freest form, and to exercise in full measure the ancient liberties and privileges of the genre.

Nor, if Byron's intent was to administer a political lesson, would he have scrambled that lesson by making his poem mock itself. Satire is given plenty of romance to feed on in *Don Juan*. If the ancient Greek romance relates "the adventures or experiences of one or more individuals in their private capacities and from the viewpoint of their private interests and emotions,"[22] Byron revives romance in this poem of adventure—revives it satirically. At least since *Don Quixote*, after all, romance has been a source of absurdity, and in *Don Juan* absurdity is richly exploited. In telling of shipwreck, slavery, and love in accordance with the oldest formulas of romance, *Don Juan* ridicules itself even as it does targets like Wordsworth. Now generating absurdities as you go serves little purpose unless the exercise of satiric liberty is itself your purpose. "Why, Man," Byron wrote to John Murray, "the Soul of such writing [as *Don Juan*] is its license; at least the *liberty* of that license, if one likes."[23] Byron's radicalism goes beyond the critique of theories and systems that imprison human life (and three-by-two sounds like the dimensions of a cell); it returns to the source from which the secular creeds of the modern age derive much of their power in the first place.

Satire, I have suggested, has an eye for the factual. It has been said that the basic style of *Don Juan*, the style to which Byron can always confidently return from his tonal flights, is that of reported fact. The reported fact simply awaits its meaning. It "can do or mean anything," depending on the direction the poem takes; it "can be put to any uses."[24] It is pure potential. In this it resembles satire itself, understood as a potential activated by literature, but also put to use, and closed down, in political doctrine.

CHAPTER 5

The Addisonian Line: Jane Austen

I n his effort to reform poetic theory and practice, Wordsworth, as we know, goes so far as to discount the difference between poetry and prose, maintaining that poetry is really metrical prose (and implying that rhyme, though statutory to the heroic couplet, is inessential to poetry as such). The poet, too, plays a more priestly role than envisioned in neoclassical theory, calling forth the humanity of those whom modern life otherwise barbarizes and alienates. "For a multitude of causes, unknown to former times, are now acting with a combined force to blunt the discriminating powers of the mind, and, unfitting it for all voluntary exertion, to reduce it to a state of almost savage torpor."[1] Though there seems to be material here for satiric complaint on the degeneracy of the age, Wordsworth goes on to associate poetry with a kind of devotional mood that has nothing of satire in it.

Among the decivilizing influences of modern life counteracted by the poet Wordsworth lists the newspaper. The newspaper jades its readers, dulling their moral powers by pandering to a "degrading thirst after outrageous stimulation," a phrase unintentionally evoking the connection of journalism with the coffee bean. The worst of the coarsening forces at work, writes Wordsworth in 1800, are

> the great national events which are daily taking place, and the increasing accumulation of men in cities, where the uniformity of their occupations produces a craving for extraordinary incident, which the rapid communication of intelligence hourly gratifies.[2]

If the quiet mood in which poetry arises, according to Wordsworth, seems contrary to the agitation of current events, so the practice of recollection opposes the journalistic emphasis on the present moment in the first place. "Daily," "hourly": Wordsworth objects to an unnatural acceleration of time or, if you will, a division of time that keeps pace with the division of labor. In contrast with this chopping up of time into days and hours at the hands of journalism, Wordsworth in the most substantial of his poems in the *Lyrical Ballads* brings out the deepening over time of his bond with Nature, as well as the continuity between the present moment and his past on the one hand and Dorothy's future on the other. Considering too that newspapers sprang up in profusion in Paris during the French Revolution (as they had in London during the English Revolution some two and a half centuries before), they were strongly associated with a cause that Wordsworth came to repudiate. The poet in any case recalls us from "the rush and roar of practical life," as Matthew Arnold would describe it.[3] Let me suggest that Jane Austen's pointed silence on the controversies of the hour—the great national events that are daily taking place—can be read in the same way, except that the novelist gets back to one of the sources of journalism itself: Addisonian satire, satire concerned to humanize the reader and advance the civilizing process.

If the Austen style, with its reduced sentimentality and controlled satiric energy, seems to reflect the tempering of emotional extremes in the course of the civilizing process (and both satire and sentimentality are apt to run to extremes), it also recalls the tasteful satires of Addison in the service of civility itself.[4] Both in Austen and Addison the relation between manners and morals is carefully modulated. Besides, it was the *Spectator* that "established the discrete unit, the limited society—whether a club, a family, or a neighborhood—that would replace the unlimited wandering of the picaro as the milieu of the novel,"[5] and in Jane Austen this miniaturization of the world finds its most aesthetically pleasing expression. Her very "Toryism" links her not indeed to Addison but to a tradition underlying him, that of estates satire.

Estates satire as we have it in the General Prologue of the *Canterbury Tales* cites the failures of the members of the several ranks to carry out the duties of their position. As Marilyn Butler points out, this is just what Jane Austen does, most markedly in the case of a gentry reproached for its failure to live up to its duty as the traditional guardian of the community.[6] (A conspicuous exception, Mr. Knightley of *Emma* has the chivalric qualities of truth and courtesy embodied in Chaucer's Knight.) The famous Austen neglect of topical issues seems itself to reflect a preference for established institutions, in this case the institution of satire. If satire is the ground from which journalism sprang, by the same token journalism may appear a newcomer, a parvenu, out of touch with tradition. Conceivably it appeared so to Jane Austen. It's possible to make too much of Austen's Toryism, though. Addison himself, a Whig, set a policy of keeping his distance from the kind of journalism that fans public passions, and presumably Jane Austen would agree with him that it is much better to be let into the knowledge of ones-self, than to hear what passes in Muscovy or Poland; and to amuse our selves with such writings as tend to the wearing out of ignorance, passion and prejudice, than such as naturally conduce to inflame hatreds and make enmities irreconcileable.[7]

Addison moderates and civilizes satire itself. In her best-loved work Jane Austen humbles a heroine given to ridicule and a hero given to scorn, satirists both. *Pride and Prejudice* is also, however, brilliantly satiric in its own right, as well as being politically the least clear of the Austen novels[8]—an indication, perhaps, that true satiric power cannot be confined within fixed political categories.

Women, says Addison, were "formed to temper mankind," not inflame public passions by taking sides in politics.[9] While Jane Austen is fortunately less amiable than Addison would like, she does temper Darcy in the sense of making him less brittle and does stay clear of public questions. Along with the circumscription of space in the Austen world goes the exclusion of hot topics like war, politics, and religion, as though the author had both an Addisonian sense of the greater importance of self-knowledge (Emma "had been entirely under a delusion, totally ignorant of her own heart")[10] and Wordsworth's sense of the barbarizing effect of journalism. Like the old master who foregrounds the plowman while in the distance a boy falls from the sky, Jane Austen keeps her focus well to the rear of the spectacular events of the Napoleonic era. The great things taking place daily and reported hourly to a sensation-starved public—all this is absent. Moments after Fanny Price is reintroduced to her father after an absence of some eight years he takes out a newspaper and "applie[s] himself to studying it, without seeming to recollect her existence."[11] The news of the world means more to him than the fact of his own long-absent child. It is one of those moments that make *Mansfield Park* such a bitter work. (Much as in Wordsworth's Preface, the newspaper is associated in the emotional economy of *Mansfield Park* with cities, demoralization, and appetite for the sensational.)[12] In and of itself, the subtlety of the Austen style administers a satiric correction to a journalistic age by *sharpening* "the discriminating powers of the mind." Clearly, absence of topicality isn't the same as absence of power. Though not concerned with the news of the day, *Pride and Prejudice* opens with news of the coming of Bingley, satirically related. Over the span of a few pages of *Emma* we read some half-dozen times of the "news" of Elton's marriage[13] and of the circulation of "information" and "intelligence" connected with it, as though the information age itself were being placed under the lens of satire. When Pope likens small things to great—Belinda dressing to a warrior being armed— the great thing doesn't really suffer by comparison. It remains undiminished.

When Jane Austen applies the language we have come to associate with great national events to the goings-on of a village, we are not so sure of the standard of comparison.

But if the local as well as the national has its news (and the circulation of the word is after all one of the concerns of the novel as a genre), then perhaps political issues can be presented by implication in local terms. Thus, while Jane Austen does not polemicize on the woman question, and while her style is contrary to the declamation and overheated rhetoric of the *Vindication of the Rights of Woman*, the portrayal of Mrs. Bennet as coquette-turned-mother bears out with silent eloquence Mary Wollstonecraft's criticism of the kind of education that teaches women to catch men and little more. So, too, it is an imbecile, Collins, who reads aloud Fordyce's Sermons, the same sermons Mary Wollstonecraft censures for "melting every human quality into female meekness and artificial grace."[14] For that matter, doesn't patriarchy itself suffer a certain deflation at Jane Austen's hands, what with the boorish General Tilney, the impotent Mr. Bennet, the infantile Mr. Woodhouse, the unconscious Sir Thomas Bertram? While there is certainly affection for established institutions in Jane Austen, her conservatism seems to allow for the undercutting of patriarchal figures, as well as mockery of the high aristocracy and officers of the established church, as it includes an affection for the institution of satire. Following Sir Thomas's halfhearted and ineffectual attempt to release his daughter Maria from a bad engagement there appears a passage of such lethal sarcasm on the institution of marriage that it is hard to imagine a radical topping it.[15] That Austen holds anything in common with critics of the existing regime is another sign of satire's power of overflowing narrow categories. She has in fact been read as both an apologist for and a critic of the conservatism that took shape in her time under the impress of the French Revolution.[16]

In suggesting that satire takes the place of topical reference in Jane Austen, I don't mean that each and every public question of the era receives a satirist's consideration. I mean that the liveliness topicality might lend a work is supplied instead by satire, that rather than placing herself at the cutting edge of the present the author uses the cutting edge of the satiric blade. The art of beheading someone and leaving them standing Jane Austen made her own. "Goldsmith tells us, that when lovely woman stoops to folly, she has nothing to do but die; and when she stoops to be disagreeable, it is equally to be recommended as a clearer of ill-fame." This of Mrs. Churchill in *Emma*, who "after being disliked for at least twenty-five years, was now spoken of with compassionate allowances," all the more because the illness she was suspected of feigning proved at last real.[17] Mrs. Churchill is known to the reader entirely by report, a topic of "news"; other grotesques we see for ourselves. There is nothing specially topical, I imagine, in the portrayal of Collins, but so brilliantly is the oaf drawn that a Gillray caricature is no more vivid. Where civility calls for carefully modulated expression and careful composition of the social self— processes analyzed to a nicety in Adam Smith's *Moral Sentiments*, whose terms by and large are also those of Jane Austen—simply to be as colossally obvious as Collins is to stand as a satiric object, a lesson in idiocy. The reticence code is already taking shape in *Pride and Prejudice*, for what makes Collins as well as his patron Lady Catherine de Bourgh so indecent is not just a seemingly complete lack of reserve, but an equal lack of regard for the reserve of Elizabeth Bennet. They both force her to be explicit. Lady Catherine, like Collins a caricature, roars and charges at her like a bull. In a world calling for subtlety it is not only the obvious, though, who say too much. Not long after she takes offense at Lady Catherine's frankness, Elizabeth taxes her own frankness, meaning the ill-advised freedom of her speech, in conversation with Darcy. In the spirit of Addison forswearing "utterances [that tend] toward the contempt, ridicule, hatred, scorn, or disrepute of other persons,"[18] she recants her excesses in telling Darcy off the preceding April. But were her criticisms of Darcy really so wide of the mark?

Not according to the one who should know. "What did you say of me that I did not deserve?" states Darcy.[19] As the author's own cuts persuade us, there is such a thing as satiric justice. In retrospect it appears that Elizabeth Bennet's exaggerated and yet just portrayal of Darcy to his own face, her satiric freedom, is exactly what started him on the way to transformation. Having done its work, such license can be abjured. Since their clash, says Elizabeth, speaking like an Addisonian, "we have both, I hope, improved in civility."[20] Unlike Lady Catherine, it seems Elizabeth Bennet has the depth necessary to reflect on her own judgment. The contrast between selves with depth and selves all on the surface lives in on fiction in the difference between a Pip and a Pumblechook, or even perhaps between Bloom (his prudence a reminder of the care that goes into the construction of the social self) and all those he runs into who it seems cannot possibly possess an inner life as abundant as his.

Masking as straight report, the classic opening sentence of *Pride and Prejudice*—"It is a truth universally acknowledged, that a single man in possession of a good fortune must be in want of a wife"—demonstrates the subtlety that a Collins sorely lacks. The General Prologue of the *Canterbury Tales*, also presented by a reporter, abounds with types who don't seem to realize that like Collins or his patron their moral deformities are on display. But the lack of realization belongs equally to our reporter, the pilgrim Chaucer, whose sense of speaking for the social consensus, for a "truth universally acknowledged," is such that he doesn't notice his absurdities and doesn't bother describing himself. It is the delicate position of Elizabeth Bennet that she possesses a lot of the satiric awareness of Chaucer the *poet*—seeing Collins for just what he is, for example—while still under deficiencies of perception and understanding, and in any case unable to remove herself to some vantage outside her small world. The pseudo-objective tone of the opening sentence registers the position of one who knows the folly of common report[21] and the social world it is the image of, but also knows there is no escape from folly. (The knowledge that he belongs to the scene he surveys with irony, that he cannot remove himself from the pageant of human life to some point in space between China and Peru—this contributes to the richness of Dr. Johnson's prose.[22] Jane Austen lets you know how vicious, risible, and yet delightful the world that you can't escape is.) Mock objectivity takes a different tone in the other line of the Chaucer tradition, as in Dickens's scathing but outwardly objective references to public opinion in *Little Dorrit*, comments that refuse to reconcile themselves in the Austen fashion to the folly and horror of things.

In the course of "the civilizing process," writes Norbert Elias, as "more and more people are being bound more and more closely together," the observation of others is heightened and acquires more nuance, while the sharper expressions of pleasure and displeasure are "moderated, contained," and generally subtilized.[23] The narrow confines of the Austen world, and the impossibility of escape, gloss the meaning of "bound." Elizabeth Bennet is the bounden daughter of Mrs. Bennet and by the end finds herself Wickham's sister-in-law. "Heightened observation" is another name for the Austen narration itself, also distinguished by the careful modulation of loathing, scorn, and glee. The play of nuance that the reader of *Pride and Prejudice* delights in from the first sentence (but which would be lost on anyone whose powers of discrimination were really blunted) records the advance of the civilizing process, as though Addison's precepts of civility had taken literary effect. Within the fictional world of Jane Austen civility seems to call for a humbling or lowering of the self, a renunciation of any sort of delusion of grandeur or vain imagining that gets in the way of consideration for others or the performance of the common obligations—the bounden duties—of life.

One such inflammation of the imagination is the kind of solipsism that overcomes Catherine Morland as a result of her habit of novel reading. In keeping with the satiric style of *Northanger Abbey*, however, Catherine's addiction calls forth from the narrator a panegyric to escapist fiction. A young lady is ashamed to be found with a novel, but had the same young lady been engaged with a volume of the *Spectator*, instead of such a work, how proudly would she have produced the book, and told its name! though the chances must be against her being occupied by any part of that voluminous publication, of which either the matter or the manner would not disgust a young person of taste; the substance of its papers so often consisting in the statement of improbable circumstances, unnatural characters, and topics of conversation, which no longer concern any one living; and their language, too, frequently so coarse as to give no very favourable idea of the age that could endure it.[24]

This of the *Spectator!* Presumably the intelligence behind the mask of folly—"A woman, especially, if she have the misfortune of knowing anything, should conceal it as well as she can"[25]—regards the *Spectator* not as an offense against taste but as a course in taste and a corrective to the "topics" of the present moment, as the light satire of ruined abbeys and haunted houses in Spectator No. 110 counteracted in its own time the fashion for gothic horror. There is after all a strong affinity between Addison and Austen, two wry observers of morals and manners, two critics whose moods range from levity to piety. If he wrote a prose "pure without scrupulosity, and exact without apparent elaboration; always equable, and always easy," as Johnson says,[26] so did she. Mr. Spectator becomes a narrator, both concealers of self. An early reviewer in fact noted, in praise of Jane Austen, that her novels convey the instruction of "the Spectator and the Rambler" all the more insinuatingly for *being* novels; though he might have added that her satire is more cutting and original than Addison's, indeed that its excess of implication is truer to the spirit of satiric overdoing, the point is well taken.[27] The very tutorial relation between the essayist and his readers is both heightened and deepened in Austen's idealization of pedagogy, of "the formation of one person's character by another, the acceptance of guidance in one's own growth,"[28] as with Mr. Knightley and Emma. The muting of political questions in Austen's works agrees too with Addison's goal and stated policy of tempering passions, political passions especially, in the interest of civic amity. And this lineage may help clarify the "substitution" of satire for journalistic immediacy in Jane Austen. For if Addison's journalism is like satire on a daily schedule—a regularity entirely consistent with the behavioral regimen called for by the civilizing process—then in her preference for satire Jane Austen reminds journalism, in a sense, of what it originally was.

"Topics of conversation which no longer concern any one living." The statement hints at the violence done to memory in consumer society, where even cultural goods are packaged and subjected to the mechanism of fashion. (In *Northanger Abbey* itself, Isabella and John Thorpe, both of them worthless, are associated with fashion: she with muslin, he with his curricle.)[29] Journalism indeed has the short life of a consumer good. It perishes with the day and is meant to do so. Satire, however, not only tends to valorize the past but, being a tradition, possesses memory of itself reaching well back in time. What is from one point of view a studied neglect of the topics of the day in Jane Austen is from another an act of remembrance, a recovery of the sources of journalism—satire itself, understood as an inheritance from the past.

Professing to report without preconceptions, journalism today nevertheless takes on something of the ready-made character of a consumer good; think only of the processing and packaging of Eyewitness News. Jane Austen, setting journalistic issues to one side, gives us characters who learn to see past their own preconceptions. The classic example is Elizabeth Bennet overcoming her prejudice against Darcy, though honorable mention goes to Catherine Morland, entrapped for a time in the gothic delusion that General Tilney's house conceals a horrific secret. (Tilney, it turns out, is not a gothic villain but a common boor, his crime not murder but incivility.) The story of a mind caught in the bonds of preconception is related satirically in both cases—in the second, indeed, in a voice exceptionally caustic. The interesting thing in Austen's fiction isn't so much what the world looks like when seen free and clear, but the trials of perception and tangles of perplexity that need to be lived through before you can see well at all. The satirist, too, it seems, takes an interest in "false consciousness."

In the case of Catherine Morland, as we know, it is a weakness for the clichés of gothic fiction that places her in a maze of error. She need only uncover the evidence to prove that Mrs. Tilney was murdered in due gothic style. A kind of fiction called gothic still survives, its formulas so set that it can be produced in quantity like the consumable it is. But maybe a closer analogy to the fiction that has taken possession of Catherine Morland's imagination, a fiction at once shocking and predictable, is the sort of story of domestic violence and sexual abuse, also shocking yet somehow formulaic, now stamped into the public imagination by infinite reiteration in the mass media. The point is not that these stories are all fictitious, but that they have been reduced to a genre in a culture where telling all has become at once a moral imperative and a successful formula, where the mass media have learned to cash in on what Jane Austen calls "the happiness of frightful news."[30] Liberated from the conventions of the past, we wind up with the conventions of tabloid television, fit only to be satirized. Perhaps Jane Austen thought the same of gothic fiction: that the very novelty of the fashion condemned it to all the absurdity of repetition that is the mark of fashion itself.

*

Jane Austen's marked silence on the issues of the day can be read as a reflection of women's exclusion from the world of public affairs. It can also, however, be taken as something eloquent and powerful in its own right, comparable to an act of speech. Again, while the exclusion of topical issues from the Austen world, and the small diameter of that world itself, convey a sense of constriction to some, we are also impressed with the free play of the author's wit—its easy moves and elegant cuts, its way of having things at its own sweet will, its supremacy. Even as the comic characters of *Emma*, Mr. Woodhouse, Mrs. Elton, and Miss Bates, repeat themselves obsessively and tie themselves up in delusion (a loss of movement Dickens will dramatize even more pointedly), the author's prose delights in its own freedom. And when Harriet Smith extols "the noble benevolence and generosity" of Mr. Knightley in asking her to dance,[31] authorial irony takes charge not only of the simpleton who is speaking but even, momentarily, of the irreproachable Mr. Knightley, whose virtue usually seems as firmly posited as the "fredom and curteisie" of Chaucer's Knight. Freedom is more properly the quality of the author's satire itself, for all its reputation of restriction.

In the sense that satire flows into different genres and is not to be confined to any one, Jane Austen in fact taps into the springs of satiric freedom. Though it might be classified generally as satiric comedy, her work doesn't so much belong to a genre as stand sui generis. Especially in *Emma* we are reminded that satire is no respecter of genres, for here it is as though *A Midsummer Night's Dream* were transposed from the stage to the pages of a novel. Lovers in a maze of mistakes; mischievous interference; a blocking agent (Mrs. Churchill); an adored ass (Elton); self-referentiality (a novel about the act of misreading, by analogy with a play staged within a play); a marriage of commoners (Harriet Smith and Robert Martin) in parallel with the marriage of nobles (Emma and Mr. Knightley); a pervading sense of "Lord, what fools these mortals be!"—it is all there. The point, of course, is the freedom of the translation; for as much as *Emma* resembles *A Midsummer Night's Dream*—itself a very free reworking of the Knight's Tale—it far more closely resembles other novels by Jane Austen.[32] *Emma* is the supreme creation of one who, rather than filling a slot in an existing genre, creates through the power of satire a virtual genre of her own.

CHAPTER 6

Dickens and Satiric Excess:
Little Dorrit

P lot—the design uniting a potentially open series of adventures—is at its
strongest in romance. The ancient Greek romance is all plot. The more
strongly plotted a story the more it tends toward romance, simply because the
coincidences, the meetings and partings, the catastrophes and deliverances
that give plots their shape derive largely from romance itself. The Latin
satire, by contrast, lacks plot entirely. A "farrago" is shapeless. So it is that
"an extraordinary number of great satires are fragmentary [or] unfinished"—
among them the *Canterbury Tales* and *Don Juan*, which are both.[1] With its false
starts, omissions, and digressions, Swift's *Tale of a Tub* seems an exhibition
of a disordered mind rather than a model of shapelessness per se, yet the
satiric energy of the work and the number of its targets seem excessive, out
of proportion to the author's presumed intention of enforcing moral truth.
The great Dickens novels, hinging as they do on coincidence and reversal, are
plotted to a fault, yet in the midst of it all is an abundance of satiric life that
seems to overflow the design itself. Satire cannot be reduced to a function of
plot in Dickens. In a sense, the force of satire asserts itself against the boundaries
that contain it, much as it once broke into the world of romance itself.[2] "It's
as if there is a deeper Dickens," writes Irving Howe, "an ur-Dickens, more
anarchic and free, who thrusts his way past the Dickens who manufactures
those tiresome plots."[3]

If the flamboyant Dickens produces tiresome plots, the reputedly tiresome Trollope took liberties with plot itself. Trollope's richer characters somehow exceed the plot that contains them and at times do pass from story to story
(so that while his novels end, they do not necessarily finish).[4] The overbalance
of character is that much more marked in Dostoevsky, whose affinity of course
lies not with Trollope but Dickens. It was Bakhtin's view that characters in

Dostoevsky "exceed [the] bounds" of plot, which is but a device to bring them into conflict and get them to speak in the first place—in effect, a means to realize the utmost freedom of speech.[5] The "plot" of the *Canterbury Tales*, which consists of a journey to Canterbury in barest outline, really is nothing more than the occasion for a clash of words,[6] and in Dickens's most comprehensively satiric work, *Little Dorrit*, a kinship with Chaucer is hinted at as early as the second chapter, where "fellow travellers" on the "pilgrimage of life" find themselves in one another's company in quarantine in Marseilles, on their way back to England.[7] The device of the pilgrimage allows Chaucer to assemble characters from different life-worlds and grants the pilgrims themselves a chance to say what they will to one and all that would never be theirs in life. Dickens by means of plot not only brings but weaves his characters together, high and low, proud and humble. As presented in the General Prologue, many of Chaucer's pilgrims seem to deform language in their own image, using their profession's terms of art. Dickens's characters, themselves deformed, tie up their speech in an extravagance of red tape, for not just the loss but the waste and perversion of freedom are a cardinal concern of this work.

It was Bakhtin's sense not only that plot in Dostoevsky enables dialogue, but that in the "polyphonic" novel pioneered by Dostoevsky characters have a power to voice ideas comparable to the author's, and even enjoy a kind of freedom in the face of the author's own designs, as strange as this may sound.[8] In *Little Dorrit*—for Bakhtin a model of satiric voicing—characters are endowed with a kind of authorial power they use against themselves. The people of *Little Dorrit* construct fictions in which their freedom is twisted and lost, such as William Dorrit's elaborate fiction of grandeur, which seems the very expression of a hopeless forfeiture. The fact of imprisonment rules over *Little Dorrit*, but imprisonment if you will in the freest sense, a state that includes not only the confinement of Mr. Dorrit in the Marshalsea but the self-imprisonment of Mrs. Clennam and the Dostoevskian Miss Wade, and in fact Mr. Dorrit's lack of mental freedom even in a state of liberty. All are entrapped by their own power of invention. William Dorrit, Mrs. Clennam, Miss Wade—such as these are the poets of a society of pretenders, a society in thrall to its own fictions. In this context satiric license means the exposure of sham and imposition, but also the reclamation at the level of narrative of the freedom tied up in these things. Like Tocqueville with his vision of the spirit "gradually broken and [the] character enervated"[9]—and William Dorrit is a broken man—Dickens's concern goes to the very springs of freedom.

The satire of *Little Dorrit* is very free, yet Dickens resented the suggestion that it was in any way extravagant. Even at its most fantastic, as in the depiction

of a Circumlocution Office at the heart of government, he insisted on its truth
to fact (in this case, the fact of a rotten Civil Service). But seeing that the
Marshalsea Prison that supplies the very symbol of *Little Dorrit* was no longer in
operation when the novel appeared, perhaps we should take fact in an extended
sense, a sense something like Carlyle's when he says

> I infer that the inner sphere of Fact, in the present England as elsewhere,
> differs infinitely from the outer sphere and spheres of Semblance. . . . For
> the substance alone is substantial; that *is* the law of Fact: if you discover not
> that, Fact, who already knows it, will let you also know it by and by! . . .
> The law of Fact is, that Justice must and will be done.[10]

In Dickens's comparable sense—and the secret at the center of *Little Dorrit*
concerns a festering injustice—fact is what resists pretense and delusion (Semblance) with satiric force. The boundless detail of *Little Dorrit* is charged with
such force, a reminder of all that cannot be imprisoned within human fictions.

The abundance of *Little Dorrit* registers a power not to be confined by
our schemes or cheated by our imaginings. The very population of the work
seems excessive. Like Chaucer, who peoples the pilgrimage not with thirty
parsons but one parson amid a human multitude, and whose fabliaux contain
satiric elements "that seem too rich for the neat basic plot,"[11] Dickens fills
his work with beings in excess of any doctrinal or literary requirement. Here
is God's plenty. Ironically, however, of this plenty many, even most, are so
pattern-bound that they almost cease to live.

Consider but a few of the multitude of grotesques in *Little Dorrit:*

- Mrs. Clennam, a figure of moral deformity exulting in her spite as
  if it were proof of divine election, and never changing. A hideous
  embodiment of both the Protestant ethic and the spirit of capitalism,
  she is summed up in these terms: "Thus was she always balancing her
  bargains with the Majesty of heaven, posting up the entries to her
  credit, strictly keeping her set-off, and claiming her due. She was
  remarkable only in this, for the force and emphasis with which she
  did it. Thousands upon thousands do it, according to their varying
  manner, every day" (p. 89). Much as Dickensian "pseudo-objectivity"
  reminds us of Chaucer's posture as a reporter of the general opinion,[12]
  in fact a reporter of the *Canterbury Tales* themselves, the portrayal of
  the singular yet typical Mrs. Clennam recalls all those in the General
  Prologue described as superlative of their kind.

- Mr. Tite Barnacle, epitome of the sinecurists and red-tape artists who populate British officialdom. "He wound and wound folds of white cravat round his neck, as he wound and wound folds of tape and paper round the neck of the country" (p. 152).
- Flora Finching of the rushing speech, her every sentence going off course; in retrospect, a kind of summation of the tradition of female garrulity before the streaming *inner* speech of Molly Bloom.[13]
- The purely superfluous John Baptist Cavalletto, "altogether a true son of the land that gave him birth" (p. 52), but as it turns out, one of a kind even in his typicality (p. 815). Cavalletto is a flourish of the author's satiric pen, an extra tangle in the fantastic forest of an illuminated manuscript, and no more necessary to the plot of *Little Dorrit* than a given stroke to a gothic design.

The overcharged detail, the detail invested with a force "greater than [its] presumed function requires," was the delight of Irving Howe.[14] The grotesques of *Little Dorrit* possess just this kind of excess: they are more numerous and realized with greater force and emphasis than the plot calls for. On this score Dickens's original biographer found fault with *Little Dorrit*. That "some of the most deeply considered things that occur in it have really little to do with the tale itself" he deemed a flaw in the work's construction.[15] It is true that Miss Wade's remarkable, and deeply considered, "History of a Self-Tormentor" interrupts rather than forwards the story of *Little Dorrit*, but the same spirit of excess that induces Dickens to add a secondary story—in the satiric tradition of the tale within the tale—also animates the work as a whole. Its plot holding things together as an overflowing cup holds its contents, *Little Dorrit* is marked from first to last by a quality of pleonasm. As suggested, the work is somehow overpeopled. (If Miss Wade is gratuitous, what of Mr. F.'s Aunt?) Among the extras are three named simply Bar, Bishop, and Physician, personifications who enact *Little Dorrit*'s satire of the high and mighty even as they evoke figures named the Man of Law, the Monk, and the Physician in the *Canterbury Tales*—Dickens himself recalling the Parson who rebukes the great and serves the poor.[16] Like Chaucer, too, Dickens seems to enter into the original sense of satire as an abundant variety.

Just as the people of *Little Dorrit* enchain themselves in fictions of their own devising, they enchain speech in the strange extravagance of circumlocution. In circumlocution, with its willful distortions, freedom of speech seems turned against itself, and we might construe *Little Dorrit* as an attempt to recover in satire the freedom thus misspent. In the spirit of satiric excess, the styles of double-talk itself exist in such abundance in *Little Dorrit* that it is impossible to read all in one way. The most noted though not necessarily the most telling example of circumlocution concerns the bureau of that name.

Tocqueville dreaded a new mode of despotism that would "enervate the soul and noiselessly unbend its springs of action."[17] Dickens depicts government working noisily to the same end, at its hub something called the Circumlocution Office—all that we know of bureaucratic shell games, he knew. The Circumlocution Office is manned by the Barnacle family, oligarchs whose business it is to obstruct, to obscure, to vex, to weary unto death, to tie up initiative in bureaucratic rites and forms, in general to work themselves round the neck of the nation like the rings of some extravagant cravat. Anyone with a project or a petition is condemned to a hopeless labor in the Circumlocution Office, "form-filling, corresponding, minuting, memorandum-making, signing, counter-signing, counter-counter-signing, referring backwards and forwards, and referring sideways, crosswise, and zig-zag" (p. 571). On the floor of Parliament the talkers-in-rings see to it that nothing gets done:

> "First, I will beg you, sir, [says a Parliamentary Barnacle] to inform the House what Precedent we have for the course into which the honourable gentleman would precipitate us;" sometimes asking the honourable gentleman to favour him with his own version of the Precedent; sometimes telling the honourable gentleman that he (William Barnacle) would search for a Precedent; and oftentimes crushing the honourable gentleman flat on the spot by telling him there was no Precedent. But Precedent and Precipitate were, under all circumstances, the well-matched pair of battle-horses of this able Circumlocutionist. (pp. 455–56)

The shift from direct to indirect discourse is characteristic of the workings of "pseudo-objective" report.

Nothing is officially done in *Little Dorrit* but on the say-so of the Circumlocution Office, meaning that nothing is officially done, period. Thus far, Dickens's analysis of institutionalized corruption differs little from that of Bentham, whose unreadable prose and scheme for building prisons make his a strange name to join with Dickens's. A proponent of reform, especially of the law, Bentham was incensed to find the very discussion of reform interdicted time and again in Parliament by the use of Barnacle tactics. Precedent and Precipitate saw action in Bentham's day, too, and he attacked that sham language with the passion of a thwarted satirist. Certainly the reformer shares the satirist's aim of both exposing and correcting wrong, even if he goes about it more literal-mindedly. In his critique of political gibberish—attacks on abuses of words are a kind of satiric constant—Bentham even sounds the satiric note: "How sweet are gall and honey! How white are soot and snow!"[18] But this is satire with a difference, satire in the process of reduction to a set of political theorems. Uncovering the motives of men, exposing the hypocrite, even quoting Horace,[19] Bentham is an ideologue assuming the liberties of the satirist. I've suggested that from the time of the French Revolution political creeds have exploited satire, confining its excess within firm boundaries and even converting its freedom to dogma. The loyalty of Dickens, who at the time of writing Little Dorrit avowed "no . . . political faith or hope,"[20] would seem to lie with satire itself as against the political doctrines that claim its arguments and its power. In the novel immediately preceding Little Dorrit, Hard Times, the Benthamite is judged a dogmatist.[21]

The Dickens-Bentham analogy extends only so far, then; and no wonder, for while the imagination had no standing with Bentham, Little Dorrit is an act of the imagination that comprehends the whole of society. Dickens after all had realized long before that "it was through the creations of his mythopoeic imagination rather than through straight journalism that he could most powerfully influence contemporary social and political attitudes."[22] Besides, what journalist would launch an attack on the Marshalsea Prison after it had already been closed and its courtyard converted (as Dickens found) to a butter shop? Dickens's indictment of the society he sought to influence is less in the spirit of Bentham than of Swift, whose hatred of financial adventurism seems to animate the Merdle sections of Little Dorrit. Like Swift, too, Dickens assumes a voice not his own and protests economic jargon in the name of Christian principles:

> Mr Merdle came home from his daily occupation of causing the British name to be more and more respected in all parts of the civilised globe capable of the appreciation of world-wide commercial enterprise and gigantic combinations of skill and capital. For, though nobody knew with the least precision what Mr Merdle's business was, except that it was to coin money, these were the terms in which everybody defined it on all ceremonious occasions, and which it was the last new polite reading of the parable of the camel and the needle's eye to accept without inquiry. (pp. 444–45)[23]

In contrast with Addison's idealization of public credit, Dickens derides the public investment of belief in an impostor. For the voice behind baroque phrases like "gigantic combinations of skill and capital" is "everybody," or a press that rhetorically speaks for everybody. In a discussion of passages like this in Little Dorrit Bakhtin remarks on Dickens's way of reporting public opinion in the style of an "admission of an objective and completely indisputable fact"—a given.[24] The device is a variation on Chaucer's pretense of reporting speech as it was given.

Published shortly after *Little Dorrit,* Mill's *On Liberty* cries out against the tyranny of public opinion (the public opinion that Arthur Clennam goes along with when he buys into what everyone is saying about Merdle) and indicts the moral and intellectual sloth of a society that believes "it is easier for a camel to pass through the eye of a needle than for a rich man to enter the kingdom of heaven," but never thinks about or acts on its creed.[25] While not arguing for a return to apostolic purity, Mill does have a nostalgic sense of origins—of a time when truths were fresh and hadn't yet declined to routine—that allies him with the republican tradition and its myth of renewal. Dickens, while also promoting a moral awakening and not a return to purity of faith as such, seems closer to Swift's position that the plain terms of the Father's will have been perverted over time. In any event Dickens's censure of the hypocritical reading of the parable in point as the "last new" reading, as though it came out in the evening paper, recalls Swift's contempt for the vain ephemera of the modern press. If only through his debt to Swift, Dickens participates in a tradition that finds in the past the very ground of the present. Measured against fiction, journalism does not reach down into human life. Through his portrayal of human character in *Little Dorrit* Dickens also seems to say that a Benthamite analysis of the circumlocution problem does not reach deep enough.

For if bombast like "gigantic combinations of skill and capital" is in the mouth of everybody, then it seems the whole of society, not just Parliament or a given bureau, is engaged in double-talk. And so it proves. In the immensity of *Little Dorrit* scarcely a human being exists who doesn't practice circumlocution in the plain sense of talking around things. Everybody does it. Perhaps the prince of the practice, though, is William Dorrit. Given to periphrastic expression and fictions of nobility, William Dorrit when he accepts alms conducts himself with the air of a king on a state occasion. Thus does the patriarch of the Marshalsea Prison beg for money from Arthur Clennam:

> A—well—a—it's of no use to disguise the fact—you must know, Mr Clennam, that it does sometimes occur that people who come here desire to offer some little—Testimonial—to the Father of the place. (p. 123)

When Mr. Dorrit becomes rich he carries his circumlocutions if anything even further. In an "epistolary communication" he

> surrounded the subject with flourishes, as writing-masters embellish copy-books and ciphering-books: where the titles of the elementary books of

arithmetic diverge into swans, eagles, griffins, and other calligraphic recre-
ations, and where the capital letters go out of their minds and bodies into
ecstasies of pen and ink. (p. 658)

Clearly an analogy is intended between William Dorrit's shams of gentility
and circumlocutions and moral enervation on the one hand, and on the
other the shams of the Circumlocution Office, itself as airless as a prison.
But at the same time, Mr. Dorrit's fictions are excused in some degree by
their sheer extravagance, by the free play of fancy in them—swans, eagles,
griffins (almost as though Dickens had in view the borders and capitals of
the Ellesmere Chaucer). Anyway, who would begrudge this pitiful Lear the
fictions to cover his nakedness? There are those today who would say that
William Dorrit needs professional help. Where Dickens writes of mind-forged
manacles, we now have an entire therapeutic culture that speaks, as he did, in
the name of humanitarianism, albeit in a language as pretentious and vacant
as any satirized in *Little Dorrit*. And being a satirist of a high order, Dickens
allows no pat judgment of William Dorrit, nor does he leave us certain how
to evaluate all of the seemingly innocent conceits and dignity-saving devices,
the fantastications and polite omissions, the acts of self-censorship and the
extravagant self-deceits that go to make up ordinary human converse in this
remarkable work. The many varieties of circumlocution in *Little Dorrit* convey
the power of satiric excess. Of some, but only some, of these displays of
complication Dickens seems to be saying, "Reason not the need!" Some of
the arabesques of speech in *Little Dorrit* seem a distorted and futile expression
of freedom.

A few other circumlocutors:

- The giddy Flora Finching talks around her wish to scold Arthur Clennam, so far around that she gets lost. She makes a beginning but ends,
  like Parliament, by not doing it.

  "Most unkind never to have come back to see us since that day,
  though naturally it was not to be expected that there should be
  any attraction at *our* house and you were much more pleasantly
  engaged, that's pretty certain, and is she fair or dark blue eyes or
  black I wonder, not that I expect she should be anything but a
  perfect contrast to me in all particulars for I am a disappointment
  as I very well know and you are quite right to be devoted no
  doubt though what I am saying Arthur never mind I hardly know
  myself Good gracious!" (pp. 313–14)

Crazier than Jane Austen's Miss Bates, if no more wordy, Flora Finching summarizes the tradition of female garrulity that Molly Bloom will ironize by her silence.

- Plornish, the plasterer, delivers a peculiarly "prolix" account of the troubles of Bleeding Heart Yard, "turn[ing] the tangled skein of his estate about and about" and getting nowhere (p. 184), his speech an effusion of futility like a game of ball in a prison yard.
- John Chivery, the doomed suitor of Little Dorrit, possesses such native delicacy of sentiment that even his imaginary epitaph on a life of sorrow contains a euphemistic omission: "Stranger! Respect the tomb of John Chivery, Junior, who died at an advanced age not necessary to mention" (p. 802).
- Mrs Gowan talks around her own mercenary motives:

> And Mrs Gowan, who of course saw through her own threadbare blind perfectly, and who knew that Mrs Merdle saw through it perfectly, and who knew that Society would see through it perfectly, came out of this form, notwithstanding, as she had gone into it, with immense complacency and gravity. (p. 444)

A social equivalent of paper shuffling.

- Mrs. General, hired by old Dorrit after his change of fortune, prefers to talk around the ungenteel question of money. When Dorrit falteringly opens the subject, she stops him in the middle of the word "remuneration." " 'It is a subject on which I prefer to avoid entering. I have never entered on it with my friends here; and I cannot overcome the delicacy, Mr Dorrit, with which I have always regarded it' " (p. 501).
- Arthur Clennam labors to keep up the fiction that he is not in love with Pet Meagles. "If Arthur Clennam had not arrived at that wise decision firmly to restrain himself from loving Pet, he would have lived on in a state of much perplexity, involving difficult struggles with his own heart" (p. 354). This is to say, in the way of circumlocution, that Arthur *did* struggle in perplexity. Clennam plays a sort of language game with himself which the author reports in accordance with the rules of satiric objectivity. The game shades into self-deceit when, in weakness of will, he acts the part of a man too old for love, one whose interest in Little Dorrit, for example, can only be fatherly. Even Clennam, for all his troubled conscience and concern for the insulted and the injured, is a kind of pretender, it seems; at least his affectation of guilt doesn't

keep him from incurring real guilt as the novel moves along. In Arthur Clennam the sensitive heart becomes an aptitude for resignation and regret, sympathy with others goes along with a lack of self, altruism is bound up with weakness of character. A lesser satirist might not have ironized his own ethos as Dickens does by making his hero such a failure. As it happens, the author's running pseudonym for Clennam is one that Odysseus uses for himself: Nobody.

When in the Eumaeus episode of *Ulysses* Bloom complains of "circumlocution departments with the usual quantity of red tape and dillydallying of effete fogeydom and dunderheads generally,"[26] Joyce may be joking at Dickens's expense, convicting him as the author of a cliché. At its origin, however, it was not a cliché, and *Little Dorrit*'s satire not only on bureaucratic procedure but characters who wrap themselves in red tape, including an effete hero, has both point and force.

As suggested, grotesques appear in *Little Dorrit* in an abundance beyond the bare needs of narration (or with the pleonasm of Bloom's complaint), and what makes them grotesques is their entrapment in fictions of their own creation—their mechanical repetition of some way of pretending that seems to have taken them over. William Dorrit, Flora Finching, Casby, all of them pretend so habitually, if also variously, that even in their intensity they seem to have lost some of the quality of living beings. They become functions of their own artifice. They strangle in their circumlocutions. They are warped images of their creator, subjecting themselves to their own power of invention where *his* power of invention outruns the constraints of plot and the simplicity of pattern.[27] Orwell, in the anti-utopian tradition, imagines humanity enslaved to ruthless political engineers: Dickens portrays characters enslaved to their own fictions, characters who have in one degree or another exchanged human life for the patterns of mechanism. The master image of the work, fittingly, is self-imprisonment: Mrs. Clennam's willed paralysis, William Dorrit's manacled mind, Merdle's trick of handcuffing himself, Miss Wade's self-created prison of spite. If the satirist's liberties illumine the meaning of free expression, Dickens satirizes those who employ their freedom only to enchain their being in blind repetition. In the Menippean tradition "the minds of men and women are created free to transcend their self-made stereotypes" but use that freedom only "to construct new ones."[28] So it is in *Little Dorrit*. The paradox of a novel of great vitality filled with characters who have more or less forsaken life is accounted for by the fact, first, that these characters have turned their own freedom against themselves and, second, that the satiric energy

of the work exceeds the constraints these self-made captives have strangely
elected.

Among the captives, special mention goes to Miss Wade, betrayed by
her own vision of a world of pretenders—her faculty of satire. Like her creator
a writer, Miss Wade opens her memoirs thus:

> I have the misfortune of not being a fool. From a very early age I have
> detected what those about me thought they hid from me. If I could have
> been habitually imposed upon, instead of habitually discerning the truth, I
> might have lived as smoothly as most fools do. (p. 725)

Consumed with resentment of supposed injuries, Miss Wade is in fact the dupe
of her own imagined power of detection. A self-tormentor, Dickens calls her,
the term itself illustrating the perversion of activity encountered so often in
Little Dorrit. As a warning both of the dangers of satiric fury and the fallacies of
satiric insight, Miss Wade is a notable example of the satirist satirized. She is
also a study in the *ressentiment* since deeply tapped by the politics of victimhood, a
politics marked by the same mix of animus and self-pity, the same conspiratorial
imaginings, the same liberation rhetoric ("I thought I would try to release the
girl from bondage" [p. 734]), the same pretense of seeing in depth. It is as if,
like a Dickens character, satire had become a mockery of itself.

*

While not a work of journalism, *Little Dorrit* in its own fashion does document
the ways of power, expose abuses and swindles, chronicle high society and peer
into the social depths, track public opinion, and offer human-interest stories—
all of them practices of the press. But beyond this, *Little Dorrit* dramatizes what
makes things worthy of report in the first place. In a sardonic analysis of the
loss of a sense of reality among the American architects of the Vietnam War,
Hannah Arendt reminds us that the facts have a way of not conforming to our
theories, calculations, "scenarios." Possessed of a managerial mentality and "an
utterly irrational confidence in the calculability of reality,"[29] many a planner
of the Vietnam War seems to have gotten lost in his models. That wouldn't
have surprised an author whose characters get stuck in their own fictions. As a
satirist Dickens knows that schemes often make captives of their own authors;
even Miss Wade, who imagines herself no one's dupe, is the hopeless captive
of her own conspiracy theory. The power of the real to confute our designs
is registered above all simply by the abundant nature of the world in *Little
Dorrit*—the characters in excess of plot; the amazing varieties of self-delusion;

the deformations of speech impossible to read in one way. It is the satirist who most richly possesses what the war planners in their defactualized world lacked. It is the satirist, with his sense of the contrary nature of things, who best grasps reality's "disconcerting habit of confronting us with the unexpected," as Hannah Arendt puts it.[30] In the *Canterbury Tales*, no sooner has the pattern for the tales been established by the Knight than the Miller breaks in from nowhere and satirically destroys it. While to economists of Swift's era it may have been an axiom, a law, that population is the wealth of a nation, in "A Modest Proposal" we are shown the only way this law could be made to apply to Ireland (and Dickens's treatment of economic dogma is in the spirit of Swift).[31] *Ulysses*, again, is so profuse with detail, and yet so tempts us to suppose they all fit in some grand design, that we search over hundreds of pages to figure out why Bloom carries around a potato. We find out, more or less, but only at the cost of missing the point that no grand design depends on a potato. With its loose ends and teeming factuality and relative plotlessness, *Ulysses* seems to satirize the very idea of cosmos that it embodies, whereas *Little Dorrit* seems to surpass its own design.

As a matter of literary fact, satire specializes in testing "ideas and generalizations and theories and dogmas over against the life they are supposed to explain."[32] From the havoc played on the written word by the life force of the Wife of Bath to Rabelaisian ridicule of scholasticism to Orwell's exposé of an ideology pretending to be the key to past, present, and future, satire speaks of the power of the real to disconcert our dearest formulas. "The satirist demonstrates the infinite variety of what men do"—hence Dickensian plenitude—"by showing the futility . . . of attempts to systematize or formulate a coherent scheme of what they do."[33] Satire may even disconcert its own patterns. So it is that amid so many mechanical beings incapable of growth in *Little Dorrit* there is one who outgrows her innocence in a way her role seemed to forbid—Little Dorrit herself. Little Dorrit outgrows being little. Toward the end of the novel as she reclaims Arthur Clennam she shows a kind of implicitly sexual forwardness that earlier seemed ruled out by her portrayal as a figure of self-abnegation. A figure takes on flesh. If Gulliver by dint of long acquaintance becomes a human being to the reader rather than a generic figure, this may or may not comport with the author's satiric intent. Leopold Bloom is so fully and indisputably human that it is hard to classify him with that stark type the cuckold and impossible to take him as a cipher for anyone else, including Odysseus. In the metamorphosis of Amy Dorrit—in her achievement of singularity—Dickens seems to bring out the poverty of formulas and schematic designs.

At some point probably every reader of Dickens has the feeling that his novels are themselves formulaic—the same oddity over and over again. Dickens's novels do constitute a virtual genre unto themselves, but this is also to say that they have nothing of the ready-made or generic quality of journalism. Drawing on the power of satire—a power independent of fixed literary genres—Dickens created in effect a genre of his own.

*

Blended into the satire of *Little Dorrit* in accordance with the singularity of the author's vision is a tale of mystery, duly resolved at the end. According to Dickens's contemporary Karl Marx, the tale of earthly existence itself is destined for resolution in communism, "the solution of the riddle of history," or alternatively democracy, "the resolved mystery of all constitutions."[34] Before the one and the other all masks fall away as if in the presence of a power that explodes error, like satire. Inasmuch as Marx deals in scorn, ridicule, and fury, and strips hypocrisy bare, he does in fact have something of the satirist in him. Yet as we hear despotisms call themselves "democratic republics" in Marx's name, we can't escape the feeling that his thought has itself proved a great source of imposture; and no wonder, perhaps, for the claim to have solved the riddle of earthly being, like Oedipus answering the Sphinx, is pure bravado. With the Marxist abuse of the term as a prime example, the language of democracy has become "the public cant of the modern world."[35] And cant calls for satire, as the cant of the press is satirized in *Little Dorrit*. In effect Dickens preserves satire against those who would bind it up in ideological formulas and abstract absolutes. With Dickens, then, satire is more than a source of rhetorical gestures: it is a writ of freedom.

CHAPTER 7

Trollope and the Moderation of Satire

Whether in an effort to break whatever remains of the influence of the Victorians or to open up new territory for commercial exploitation, consumer society stages frequent raids on the last few outposts of reticence. It is sometimes implied that Victorian reticence was even a conspiracy of silence. In one cardinal respect this characterization is untrue: the precepts of reticence were themselves discussable.[1] Trollope's *The Prime Minister* (1876) opens with a discourse on the sometimes painful necessity of concealing a common background—"And yet it is difficult to be altogether silent!"—as well as the "unfortunate publicity" surrounding the club man who talks too much.[2] In the course of the novel a journalist mounts a public attack on the prime minister that violates the code of reticence as impudently as Ferdinand Lopez, a Jewish adventurer, breaks the gentleman's agreement of Victorian civility.[3] In *The Way We Live Now* (1875) the crowning disgrace of Melmotte, a financial charlatan of the magnitude of Merdle in *Little Dorrit*, is to attack a fellow MP by name on the floor of the House of Commons in violation of the rules and customs of that body. I want to suggest that Trollope, a sometimes satirist himself, finds in satire a potential for the same excess and crudity shown by the journalist on the one hand and the boor on the other. To say that "Trollope is not Jonathan Swift, and humour rather than savage indignation" marks his satiric style, is also to say that he belongs to the line of Addison rather than the tradition that comes to Swift through Rabelais and passes to Smollett and Dickens.[4]

With *Little Dorrit*, indeed, Dickens became a sore point with Trollope. Denying that he patterned Melmotte on Merdle, he went so far as to claim, falsely, that he had never read *Little Dorrit* before writing *The Way We Live Now*. He not only read it, he resented it. As a postal inspector, Trollope took offense at Dickens's caricature of the Civil Service, under the figure of the Circumlocution Office, as a brotherhood of do-nothings. "Then comes the popular novelist," he wrote in *The Three Clerks* in 1857, "and, with his sledge hammer, gives [the Civil Service] the last blow, and devotes every mother's son in the public offices to lasting ignominy and vile disgrace."[5] It's as if Trollope felt dishonored, as if he could not read—however well he could write—as an Addisonian, but must take personally what was not personally intended. The retort to Dickens was dropped from all later editions of *The Three Clerks*. Perhaps it was in a similar spirit of misgiving at having said too much that Trollope more or less retracted the satire of *The Way We Live Now* in the end, too. Satiric license called forth an ambivalence in Trollope.[6] In the one case he resented it only to regret, apparently, his own intemperance, in the other exercised it himself only to issue a kind of Chaucerian disclaimer after the fact.[7] Ambivalence seems written into *The Way We Live Now* itself, a satire so cutting it offended reviewers[8] and yet so qualified that the old question of who will marry whom takes over the work. Maybe Trollope was seeking the classic balance of satire and civility—of mordancy and sweetness—in Jane Austen, who also tells love stories and whose most enjoyed work, *Pride and Prejudice*, he considered the finest novel in the language.

*

If satire and journalism are relatives however estranged, as I have proposed, we might expect Trollope's criticism of the one to shade into criticism of the other. And so it does. With its equipoise of the serious and the comic, the said and the unsaid, indeed satire and softness, Trollope's very style seems a comment on something as ill modulated as modern journalism. With Henry James, who did much to establish the image of Trollope as a mediocrity, we feel this even more strongly; we feel that the fineness of his style reflects on the coarseness of instruments like the press, all the more because of his thematic concern with the charlatanism of publicity (as in *The Bostonians*) and his portrayal of the journalist as violator. But Trollope too unmasks the journalist. Like James's Flack a purveyor of scandal, Quintus Slide in *The Prime Minister* is a figure of ugliness— one who not only lacks the delicacy of the true gentleman but tortures a prime minister whose delicacy is his affliction. With a show of virtue Slide writes an article in the *People's Banner* placing the prime minister in the agonizing position of either exposing the conduct of his wife to public comment, which his sense of reticence forbids, or maintaining a lie. That Slide's allegations are "at any rate true to the letter" makes them more vile to Trollope.[9] In this case, it seems, the truth of a libel is not only no defense but an aggravation of the crime, in that it gives the attacker cover even as he goes about stripping away the kind of cover that makes life civil and decent. A figure of leering indecency, Slide is portrayed by the author in a special satiric register. In possession of information to use against the duke, he "stroked his hand over his mouth and chin as he sat thinking of the tremendous national importance of this communication. The man who had paid the money [for the election expenses of Lopez] was the Prime Minister of England,—and was, moreover, Mr. Slide's enemy!"[10] With invisible quotation marks around *tremendous national importance* indicating that "these are his words and not mine" (a shift of voice that marks the workings of satiric objectivity), the author exposes the exposer—reveals him as one who not only disguises a private cause as a public one but believes his own masquerade. There is still some poison in Trollope's pen. In the tradition of Addison's criticism of "the other public prints" for fanning political passions,[11] Trollope exposes a journalist who tries to work the nation into a passion as false as his own.

Mr. Alf, editor of the *Evening Pulpit* in *The Way We Live Now*, isn't the vulgarian Slide is, but still an enemy of civility—and this because a satirist. Alf abuses simply everybody, hiding behind the pretense of impartiality where Slide takes cover behind the facts. By caricaturing one and all, Alf keeps up sales without making any of his targets feel singled out, a policy that reads like a perversion of Addison's.

> Mr. Alf had . . . discovered another fact. . . . Censure from those who are always finding fault is regarded so much as a matter of course that it ceases to be objectionable. The caricaturist, who draws only caricatures, is held to be justifiable, let him take what liberties he may with a man's face and person. It is his trade, and his business calls upon him to vilify all that he touches.[12]

Behind the seeming neutrality of the report we pick up the author's objection to the "trade" of befouling others. Now Alf, like Lopez and Melmotte, who have enough shame to commit suicide and not an ounce more, is a Jew. "The ridiculing of an outsider from the security of a conservative, order-conscious society is one of the most pervasive conventions of satire," observes Ronald Paulson.[13] Hence the treatment of Jewish interlopers by Trollope. On the other hand, satire too heated starts to resemble the outsider's resentment, and so it is, perhaps, that Trollope tempers his satire with a subtle levity and the appearance of neutrality. Alf himself is satirized with Addisonian ease:

> He had been blackballed at three or four clubs, but had effected an entrance at two or three others, and had learned a manner of speaking of those which

had rejected him calculated to leave on the minds of hearers a conviction that the societies in question were antiquated, imbecile, and moribund. . . . And that which he so constantly asserted, or implied, men and women around him began at last to believe,—and Mr. Alf became an acknowledged something in the different worlds of politics, letters, and fashion.

He was a good-looking man, about forty years old, but carrying himself as though he was much younger, spare, below the middle height, with dark brown hair which would have shown a tinge of grey but for the dyer's art. . . . He dressed with the utmost simplicity, but also with the utmost care.[14]

Here then is the Addisonian middle style. But here also is Chaucer. A Canterbury pilgrim has been transposed to the pages of a novel. The exposé of the man's game (recalling the Merchant who—like Melmotte—so advertises his own solvency that people believe it); the telltale allusion to "the dyer's art"; the implied comment on all those who take such a pretender at his word; the seeming artlessness of the entire job—all are just as Chaucer would have done. The satiric artistry of the General Prologue reappears, with Chaucer's reporting becoming Trollope's documentation of "the way we live now." (And where Trollope's "we" does not seem to include the lower classes,[15] only in the abstract and voiceless figure of the Plowman does the peasantry appear in the Canterbury group, which as Dryden says represents "the whole English nation" in Chaucer's age. Even Trollope's omission is Chaucerian.) Just as the pilgrim Chaucer seems to report the views of a credulous society that takes most at their own estimate, even as he slips in the occasional detail that people would never reveal about themselves, Trollope reports what the world believes of Alf as he reveals his use of hair dye.

As we know, Addison too stands in the tradition of the General Prologue, and like Addison Trollope wants to press satire into the service of civility. But this also means that he has reservations concerning the nature of satire—reservations so deep, in fact, that he was moved to disown the excesses of *The Way We Live Now* even while maintaining that the intention behind the work was honest and the effect, in the main, "powerful and good." It's as though the very strength of the satire were cause for apology. "The book has all the fault which is to be attributed to almost all satires, whether in prose or verse," he writes in his *Autobiography*. "The accusations are exaggerated. The implied vices are coloured, so as to make effect rather than to represent the truth."[16] The contrast with Dickens couldn't be sharper. In the preface to the first edition of *Little Dorrit* Dickens is so far from apologizing for satiric excesses that he pours scorn and ridicule—satire, in a word—on objections to the "exaggerated fiction," the "extravagant conception," the "preposterous fancy" of his novel.

He insists *Little Dorrit* is true to fact—that Merdle is no more a swindler than his original, the Circumlocution Office no more a maze of malfeasance than the Civil Service itself.[17] Sometimes only too much is enough, Dickens might have said; and he would have been right. At this date who will deny that Dickens's portrayal of bureaucracy, as colored as it is, contains a truth distinctly absent from all descriptions of this institution as "rational" or efficient or what have you? ("The chains of tormented mankind are made out of red tape," wrote Kafka.)[18] Yet Trollope does have a satiric sense of the vanity of system and design, "a sense that genuine life is to be found only outside all pattern,"[19] as shown perhaps most notably in the passage of his characters from novel to novel as though the very formulas of narrative closure were too narrow and endings were really but pauses in the flow of experience.[20] Out of a feeling that experience exceeds our models of it come characters like Plantagenet Palliser, later prime minister, who overflow the work that contains them. As it happens, the prime minister discovers to his pain that the art of government is how not to do it, quite as Dickens said. Trollope also knew the virtue of satiric license. That he appreciated satire's power to capture a truth that otherwise eludes us is clear from the fact that he used it to document the very spirit of the age in his lengthiest work (a work, too, with the Dickensian quality of being "choked with characters").[21] He disavowed it, ambiguously, all the same.

This act, reminiscent of Chaucer's retraction—but not destruction or recall—of the more colored tales, is really a disclaimer on top of a disclaimer, for within *The Way We Live Now* satire itself is criticized. Alf, after all, habitually speaks in a "mildly satirical way" (p. 731), a description that reflects uneasily on the author's own practice. The fact is that satire is both asserted and retracted in *The Way We Live Now* (as Arnold both invokes and disclaims Swift in *Culture and Anarchy*—invokes him with "sweetness and light" and disclaims him for his lack of sweetness). Thus, for example, in spite of his own portrayal of the Jew Melmotte as a tower of fraud, and of the Jew Lopez in *The Prime Minister* as a ruthless adventurer, in spite of his description of Mr. Breghert, another Jew, as "a fat, greasy man" with eyes "set too near together in his face for the general delight of Christians,"[22] Trollope ends up repudiating anti-Semitism by assigning it to an oaf, Mr. Longstaffe. When Breghert gives an honest account of his transactions with Longstaffe's daughter, it is too much for the tact of the Christian—"'Perhaps, on so delicate a subject the less said the soonest mended,'" he says (p. 727), as if the author were both parodying the code of reticence and disowning the caricature of Jews in the code's name—and upon Breghert's departure it is revealed that the real grotesque is Longstaffe himself.

As soon as he was gone Mr. Longstaffe opened the door and walked about the room and blew out long puffs of breath, as though to cleanse himself from the impurities of his late contact. He told himself that he could not touch pitch and not be defiled! How vulgar had the man been, how indelicate, how regardless of all feeling, how little grateful for the honour which Mr. Longstaffe had conferred upon him by asking him to dinner! Yes,—yes! A horrid Jew! Were not all Jews necessarily an abomination? (p. 727)

Again the use of implied quotation marks to distance the reported words from the author's own. Thus is the anti-Semitism that helps propel the satire of *The Way We Live Now* disclaimed. In a sense, satire itself is disclaimed.

A theme of Roman satire is the degeneracy of the times, a complaint seemingly implied in the very title of *The Way We Live Now*. The true gentleman of *The Way We Live Now*, the antithesis of figures like Melmotte (and of settled residence and known antecedents, unlike Melmotte), is Roger Carbury. Roger Carbury is such a rock of truth in this novel that when he deplores the corruption of the age after the example of the old satirists his accusations might almost be taken for the author's own. Melmotte, he declares, is

"a failure, whether rich or poor,—a miserable imposition, a hollow vulgar fraud from beginning to end,—too insignificant for you and me to talk of, were it not that his position is a sign of the degeneracy of the age. What are we coming to when such as he is an honoured guest at our tables?" (p. 452)—

a judgment that Trollope himself would seem to share. So, too, in his defense of Horace in the same scene Carbury might almost be speaking for an author whose own virtues as a satirist, notably his urbanity and observant eye, are of the Horatian kind. Carbury's temper is really like Juvenal's, though, seeing that like the Juvenalian Darcy in *Pride and Prejudice* he "judges society . . . by the standards of his ancestors and of tradition."[23] As Jane Austen ironizes the satiric gloom of Darcy, so does Trollope that of Roger Carbury—without, however, rewarding him in love.[24] In context, indeed, Roger's sour lament on things in general reflects the failure of his pursuit of his own cousin Hetta in particular. Looking at the world through the eyes of a disappointed lover, Roger sees, not things as they are in their native ugliness, but a projection of his own embitterment. The satire is on him, as it turns out. The bishop conversing with him "was not hopelessly in love with a young lady, and was therefore less inclined to take a melancholy view of things in general than Roger Carbury. To Roger everything seemed to be out of joint" (p. 455), including the times.

It is as though Trollope inverted Swift, so that instead of the reader of satire seeing the deformity of everyone but himself, the satirist creates a deformed world in his own image.[25]

Unless the satire of *The Way We Live Now* were somehow blunted, it might delegitimize the social order itself. As a novelist Trollope does take a skeptical view of the world, but much as Jane Austen tempers her irreverence with an acceptance of existing institutions, Trollope qualifies his satiric insight with an endorsement of things as they are. The resulting moderation contributes to the middling quality of his prose. Skepticism without cynicism: this seems to be Trollope's note. Maybe it was a sense of skirting too close to the cynical, of missing his note, that led Trollope to complicate the satire of *The Way We Live Now* with a certain ridicule of bilious gloom. Some of the sting is thus taken out of his own satire on the degeneracy of the age. In fact, just as he defuses Roger's tirade by reducing it to a lover's moaning, he softens the satiric content of the work as a whole by subordinating it to a love story. (Somewhat similarly, Henry James lays down the arms of satire in bringing *The Reverberator* to a close; the work ends like a romantic comedy.) As I have said, the great preoccupation of *The Way We Live Now*, the driving force of the plot, is the question of how the lovers will pair up. Satire is diluted with romance in something like the way the marriage question, posed so satirically by the Wife of Bath, is brought to a close in the Franklin's Tale of romance—a tale whose ethic of politic compromise resembles Trollope's own. The novelist's belief in equality as ideal rather than dogma may recall, too, the vision of an equality of man and woman projected, if also betrayed, in the Franklin's Tale.[26]

Orwell, in referring to himself somewhat fantastically as a Tory anarchist, puts us in mind of the plenitude of a satiric tradition whose mix of attack and defense, radical questioning and common sense, would be broken down into modern political doctrines. Trollope's label for himself is also a contradiction in terms, although, in keeping with his more moderate style, not as flaming as Orwell's. Trollope is "an advanced conservative liberal." As an advanced conservative liberal Trollope believes in the gradual narrowing of the gap between high and low, rich and poor, as though the duke of Omnium and his servants might one day meet as equals. The conservative liberal is

alive to the fact that these distances are day by day becoming less, and he regards this continual diminution as a series of steps toward that human millennium of which he dreams. He is even willing to help the many to ascend the ladder a little, though he knows, as they come up towards him, he must go down to meet them[27]—

a secular version of Addison's scale of being, with the middle spaces in both instances being filled in. It is true that in Addison's vision of the gradation of being as "a ladder, with an infinite number of rungs," traffic goes only one way: up.[28] Nonetheless, the spirit of Trollope's ideal is certainly Addisonian. Addison envisions the unending progress of souls toward God, with the human soul in time becoming cherubic even as the cherubs themselves advance in the scale of being, all moving toward perfection in unison. The vision of eternal progress appealed to Addison in part "because it rid the picture of the Scale of Being of that look of irremediable inequality which it had in its usual form,"[29] just as the vision of secular progress mitigated the harshness of present inequality for Trollope. But while progress takes place "day by day," it obeys no journalistic schedule and its changes are too subtle for the crude instruments of the press to measure: this seems implied in Trollope's account of progress working almost imperceptibly under the noise of politics. The really consequential changes take place over the long term. "I think that men on the whole do live better lives than they did a hundred years ago," says the bishop to Roger Carbury. "There is a wider spirit of justice abroad, more of mercy from one to another, a more lively charity, and if less of religious enthusiasm, less also of superstition" (p. 454). That the religious are less fanatic and more charitable would please Addison.

For now inequality remains so severe that it cannot even be contemplated without pain. But even though, or perhaps because, "we do not understand the operations of Almighty wisdom, and are therefore unable to tell the causes of the terrible inequalities that we see,"[30] it behooves us to perform the duties of our station. And here Trollope's morality recalls the satiric tradition. The advice given to Lucian's Menippus to do the work at hand; Candide's "we must cultivate our garden"; Conrad's ethos of work (enveloped in a mood of satire)—all are cognates of Trollope's morality, however different in tone and shading. Though we might no sooner place him among the satirists than Trollope next to Voltaire, Adam Smith reaches heights of sardonic eloquence in his survey of human folly. And he too espouses a work ethic. The case of Smith bears on Trollope in several respects: not just because he too is a kind of conservative liberal with ties with the Addisonians (citing Addison in his lectures on rhetoric, for example), nor only because he calls for fair play where Trollope upholds "the rules of the game,"[31] but because he too looks with some irony on the distinction of ranks and indeed contributes to the moderation of satire by "liberalizing" the harsh satiric conceit of the agent who serves an end beyond his intention or even ken.[32] Furthermore, although Smith's thought resembles that of one of the most roguish and reviled authors of his century—Mandeville—he himself joined in the censure of this satirist[33] and on the basis of similar insights raised a philosophy not of scandalous paradox but of civility and decorum. Where Smith corrects Mandeville, Trollope refines satire itself— tempering the excesses of the seriocomic into an even style that is serious but not too serious and keeping clear of the kind of satiric intensity that disfigures the page of Swift and darkens that of Conrad. At that, he came to think he allowed his pen too much license in *The Way We Live Now*. Evidently feeling that the task of faithful reporting called for a style at once more easygoing and more restrained, closer as it were to the Addisonian model of journalism itself but also closer to his own norm, Trollope regretted the liberties taken in his most ambitious work.

When Gulliver, returned to Europe, camps in his stable because he cannot endure the presence of a human being, we sense Swift's satire turning upon itself, as though the author felt some stirrings of regret over the extremity of his indictment of European civilization. Satire seems to beget its own modes of misgiving and retraction.[34] Trollope's regret for the satiric exaggerations of *The Way We Live Now* reminds us a little of Chaucer's recantation of those of the *Canterbury Tales* that "sownen into synne." We turn now to an author who, instead of repenting of satire in the tradition of Chaucer, radicalized it.

CHAPTER 8

Ulysses: *The Art of Surfeit*

T he reader of Trollope takes pleasure in receiving the confidences and discerning the implications of the narrator. The reader of *Ulysses* finds the decorum of narration in ruins and runs up against a kind of authorial trickery that both teases and mocks comprehension. According to Trollope, "There should be no episodes in a novel," nothing to get in the way of the story.[1] *Ulysses*, constructed in episodes, barely has a story. With its implication of a great power sinking into decadence, Trollope's most satiric work has certain classical overtones. *Ulysses* resonates with a still more ancient story whose hero's virtues are not Roman. If Trollope flirts with anti-Semitism, Joyce ennobles even as he ridicules a Jew, Bloom. If Trollope's vision of gradual progress stretches out time (and realism itself modifies the journey through space into one through time), *Ulysses* condenses all the years of Odysseus' return into a single day in June of 1904. If Trollope has the satiric touch of the General Prologue of the *Canterbury Tales*, Joyce's kinship is more with the tales themselves, tales presented in a variety of voices, winding around the theme of adultery, dominated by the Wife of Bath—precursor of Molly Bloom—and excused by a jesting author in terms later employed in the decision admitting *Ulysses* into the United States and solidifying the legal basis of freedom of expression.[2]

In presenting himself as the mere recorder of the *Canterbury Tales*, Chaucer seems to waive the glories of authorship—glories that Dante claimed in casting himself as successor of Virgil. Chaucer's judgments on his fellow mortals are also less definitive and in fact less stated than Dante's on the inhabitants of Hell. In many respects an anti-Dante, Chaucer declines to heroize himself and rejects "the epic aspiration as the defining characteristic of the great writer."[3] Joyce, not given to Chaucerian humility, seems to make the conquest of epic a test of his greatness. The very concepts of epic and hero are in any case leveled in *Ulysses*. Joyce gives the impression of one immortalizing the city and citizens of Dublin in the manner of Dante placing his contemporaries under the aspect of eternity, so that every detail takes on figural meaning in a great design, but this is Dante with an inflection of irony, a subversive difference. Not only is the ethos of *Ulysses* that of Bloom, who abjures both sword and fire, not only does the work possess a satiric excess overflowing any principle of design, but it is of this world and no other. In place of Dante's vertical universe, Joyce depicts a city-world where all things exist on a common plane. Abstractly speaking, *Ulysses* thus has a good deal in common with a newspaper's "cross-section of a single day where the most diverse and contradictory material is laid out . . . side by side,"[4] again as in Chaucer. But by the same token, *Ulysses* is like no newspaper that ever was.

*

Since Chaucer posed as a reporter and one of my concerns is with the underpinnings of journalism, it may be fitting, before moving on to *Ulysses*, to glance at a story in *Dubliners* with a newspaper article at its center. Told with hints of stifled passion and evocative of more than it says, "A Painful Case" concerns James Duffy, a bank clerk who is something of an imaginary Zarathustra, and his failed liaison with a married woman, Mrs. Sinico. Four years after the clerk breaks off with her rather than surrender his isolation and heroic rarity, his eyes fall on an account in the evening paper of Mrs. Sinico's suicide.

A PAINFUL CASE

To-day at the City of Dublin Hospital the Deputy Coroner (in the absence of Mr Leverett) held an inquest on the body of Mrs Emily Sinico, aged forty-three years, who was killed at Sydney Parade Station yesterday evening. The evidence showed that the deceased lady, while attempting to cross the line, was knocked down by the engine of the ten o'clock slow train from Kingstown, thereby sustaining injuries of the head and right side which led to her death.

James Lennon, driver of the engine, stated that he had been in the employment of the railway company for fifteen years. On hearing the guard's whistle he set the train in motion and a second or two afterwards brought it to rest in response to loud cries. The train was going slowly. . . .

The jury returned a verdict in accordance with the medical evidence and exonerated Lennon from all blame.

The Deputy Coroner said it was a most painful case, and expressed great sympathy with Captain Sinico and his daughter. He urged on the railway company to take strong measures to prevent the possibility of similar accidents in the future. No blame attached to anyone.[5]

As if in compliance with some Chaucerian policy of reporting words just as they were uttered, Joyce reports at painful length an account so factual it approaches the grotesque. The very title of the story is quoted.

The suicide of Mrs. Sinico evokes the image of Anna Karenina, of an uncomprehending husband like Charles Bovary, in any event of some story that transcends the blank poverty of the newspaper account. But about that story we know next to nothing. In its formality the inquest is like a grid laid over an archaeological site, fixing the shards and scraps that are all that remains of a way of life. The point is what isn't there. If something becomes a case by an act of abstraction, an erasure of human detail, the show of the inquest simply closes the case of Mrs. Sinico as though her death were some kind of generic event like an industrial accident. The imposition of bureaucratic forms on her death—the denial of liability, the automatic classing of a singular event among "similar" ones not yet in existence—powerfully enforces a traditional satiric point, namely that systems are out of touch with the facts of experience. (In and of itself the dead-end conclusion, "No blame attached to anyone," points an affinity with the Dickens line of the satiric tradition. The original title of *Little Dorrit* was *Nobody's Fault.*) In truth, through the entire article, so scrupulously factual and so dutifully quoted, runs an undercurrent of the outrageous. Reading it is something like reading the also scrupulously dry and eerily bureaucratic "Modest Proposal"—your eardrums splitting from "loud cries."[6] If Swift impersonates the reasonable man with lethal effect, Joyce, an unsurpassed mimic of voices, offers an imitation of journalism so absolute it reads like the extremity of satire.[7]

In *Ulysses* press clippings are used with a literalism perhaps even more parodic, at times reminding us of scraps of newsprint pasted onto a collage, signifying nothing. The image of the exiled Joyce poring over Dublin newspapers for use in *Ulysses* has entered scholarly lore. Yet what the *Irish Independent*, the *Freeman's Journal*, and their fellows supplied *Ulysses* turns out in many cases to be some odd detail that stands out simply for its superfluousness. As Simon Dedalus encounters Dilly in "Wandering Rocks," bicycle racers go speeding by:

> Bang of the lastlap bell spurred the halfmile wheelmen to their sprint. J. A. Jackson, W. E. Wylie, A. Munro and H. T. Gahan, their stretched necks wagging, negotiated the curve by the College Library. (p. 227)

Race and racers were taken straight from the newspapers, a factual flourish. Of Father Conmee in the same episode it is incidentally reported that he cleaned his teeth "with arecanut paste" (p. 211). Advertisements for Areca Nut toothpaste appear in the *Daily Express* of June 17, 1904.[8] Bicycle racers, toothpaste:

details like these are throwaways, pure excess, practically Rabelaisian filler serving the design of *Ulysses* not at all but contributing to the fullness of its life. As though it were being reminded of its own precursor, journalism thus assists in making *Ulysses* a satire in the original sense of an abundance. As applied to the portrayal of the Blooms, the satiric principle of excess means that the stock figures of wronged husband and errant wife are so enriched, endowed with such overflowing ("superfluous") being, that they are no longer stock at all. Just as the wealth of information as well as allusion in *Ulysses* exceeds the requirements of any imaginable structural scheme, the wealth of life in Leopold and Molly Bloom exceeds the schematic types that underlie them. Cuckold and adulteress both overfulfill their type because they possess in abundance the human detail absent from the case of Mrs. Sinico. The report of Mrs. Sinico's death is words. The Blooms are words made flesh.

In making our way to the Blooms, let us look more closely at the satiric technique of objective report.

Concerning the portrayal of Lopez in *The Prime Minister* John McCormick observes that there remains in a reader's mind "the unresolved question as to whether Trollope believed that he was uncritically reflecting current attitudes, in keeping with his career-long portrayal of manners, or whether he was using Lopez to fix attention on anti-Semitism and so by inference to revile it."[9] Does Trollope passively register or actively satirize the anti-Semitism of such a one as Mr. Abel Wharton, Q.C., when that gentleman refers to Lopez aloud as a "Jew-boy" and in his mind as a "swarthy son of Judah"?[10] The insolubility of this riddle marks another Chaucerian affinity, for on many questions Chaucer's use of screens and habits of caution leave the reader in a kind of final uncertainty. And in the portrayal of the Wife of Bath, the dominatrix of the *Canterbury Tales* and a lot closer to Molly Bloom than Penelope, the ambiguities are at their most acute. When Chaucer portrayed the Wife in the very terms so dear to antifeminism—as a devourer of men, a liar and insatiable babbler, ungovernable, perverse, scarlet—was he satirizing antifeminism itself, mocking it with a monster of its own imagination, implying that it even creates the thing it most dreads? Does the Wife of Bath fulfill the terms of misogyny too well? Is she painted too bright, like a decoy? Does Chaucer mirror or parody the powerful tradition of antifeminism? No matter how strong our wish to do credit to Chaucer by answering "parody," the question can never be decided. Even if the poet's intent was to ridicule the antifeminists for the very lack of reason they impute to women, the Wife can still be read the other way, thanks to his policy of self-concealment. Unwittingly enforcing the traditional satiric point that fools can never evade their own folly, the Wife (you might conclude) simply demonstrates her moral errancy with every show of knowledge and every affirmation of self. How can we tell this reading is mistaken? In the case of Moll Flanders the equivalent issue is to what degree the author is at one with his heroine, to what degree he holds her up as an object lesson. Even Flaubert, for that matter, let his attorney argue that Emma Bovary was intended as an object lesson—Flaubert, who famously "is" Emma Bovary. With Molly Bloom the entire question of approbation seems to pass into irrelevance. Her husband is as sure to trigger the identification of Jews with, say, humanitarianism, lack of nationality, and sexual perversion as the Wife of Bath to trigger her critics the antifeminists. The point is, of course, how far Bloom transcends a bigot's cartoon. And so it is with Molly Bloom. Molly Bloom individualizes the most scandalous and satirized traits of Woman too completely to be an example of anything. A number of Canterbury pilgrims are depicted as so superlatively typical of their craft or class that they are one of a kind ("Ne was ther swich another pardoner"). In Molly Bloom such uniqueness is not asserted rhetorically but realized in fact.

Even in her uniqueness, however, Molly Bloom attests to the Wife of Bath. Both in the mighty torrent of her speech and in its moods, from sweet nostalgia to bitter combat, and indeed in its most general feature—the strong use of the first person—as well as in many particulars, her monologue calls up the Wife's, although in this case traditionally satirized traits like excessive desire are embodied too richly for the character to be taken for a cartoon of any kind.[11] Woman hatred is left to that cleric Deasy. ("A woman brought sin into the world" [p. 34].) With Joyce, it seems, the question isn't "mirror or parody?" because mirror *is* parody. As in "A Painful Case," faithful imitation turns to infidelity. One speaks after all of cunning resemblance. Not only because he follows Wordsworth in revealing the ordinary does Joyce deserve a place in M. H. Abrams's account of the romantic revolution, with its turn from mirror to lamp.[12] He deserves a place because he revolutionizes the mirror itself, converting it to an instrument of satire. Such is Joyce's overthrow of the mirror model that he confounds the traditional priority of the original over the copy (the *Odyssey* and its hero over *Ulysses* and its hero), Nature over art, the symbolized over the symbol.

There is a lot of joking in antifeminist satire, and it's entirely possible that the standard topics appear in Book III of *Gargantua and Pantagruel* in all of their overfamiliarity not because the author deems women treacherous and insatiable but simply because the topics supply material. (Certainly the Woman Question furnished material to Chaucer: he wrote on both sides of it.) Joyce, it seems to me, materializes Woman herself. Let me suggest that in the Rabelaisian world of *Ulysses* Molly Bloom is Woman fleshed—fleshed to the point that she not only fulfills but outdoes the traditional image of Woman from Juvenal, and before, to modern times. The reader encountering Molly Bloom may feel, "Here is an archetype, a symbol," but this particular symbol takes precedence over the thing it is supposed to symbolize. Molly Bloom, that is, so realizes traits like wandering desire traditionally satirized in Woman that she cannot be reduced to a mere instance, a "case" painful or not, and probably cannot even be placed within ready-made moral categories; at least her husband, who knows her best, never does so.

In contrast with the sterility of stereotypes in general, satiric types, seemingly by virtue of their own history, possess a potential for life. Enriched by their lineage, they sometimes take on flesh and voice in a way that distinguishes them from stark abstractions and enables them to outgrow, as it were, their own definition. A paradigm case is once again the Wife of Bath, who even in her derivation from the old procuress of the *Romance of the Rose* possesses the life of a unique being, a life attested by the force of her voice. So it is with Molly Bloom, whose name recalls, and herself recollects, Moll Flanders—a transfiguration of the also five-times-married Wife of Bath. Over the distance of centuries (and as if through the mediation of Moll Flanders) Molly Bloom bears witness to the Wife of Bath as powerfully as the Wife does her own much closer original and achieves complete singularity in her own right as the Wife does.

Chaucer reports "everich a word" of the pilgrims' tales, Joyce every word of Molly Bloom's monologue. And where Chaucer transcribes La Vieille into the Wife of Bath—the great monologuist of the *Canterbury Tales*—Joyce effectually transcribes the Wife into Molly Bloom. From her resentment that men "can pick and choose . . . but were to be always chained up" (p. 726) to her hope of "get[ting] in with a handsome young poet at my age" (p. 725) to her notion that "itd be much better for the world to be governed by the women in it" (p. 727), Molly Bloom's musings are the Wife's all over again, now voiced in the mind alone. The immediate source of one "Mrs Maybrick that poisoned her husband" by putting arsenic in his tea (p. 696) is the newspapers; but the story also calls up the list of murderesses, including some who gave their mate "poysoun in hire drynke," cited by the Wife of Bath's last husband.[13] (The men of both of these women find themselves a term in a series.) Where the Wife, with her loud clothes and loud voice, defies the ancient prohibition on women making themselves public, Molly Bloom as a singer defies the traditional condemnation of women appearing on stage. The Wife, again, has a way of beginning statements with an arbitrary "for," Molly with "because," both terms bearing sexual meaning.[14] The resemblance between the two soliloquists goes deeper, though, than the virtually direct echoes of the Wife's word that we seem to hear, extending to the spirit of the act. In Molly Bloom we meet the same somehow affirmative spirit of polemic, accusation, and complaint found in the Wife of Bath. Like a true descendant of the Wife, Molly Bloom keeps on arguing even in her own mind, as if the act of argument were released from all function and has become pure self-expression. Chaucer realizes the Wife of Bath rather than simply defining her as an object of reprobation. Molly is realized so completely that she seems to moot reprobation itself.

As we know, *Ulysses* calls itself a "chaffering allincluding most farraginous chronicle" (p. 402). The Wife of Bath's Prologue, with its argumentative play and its commercial terms and tenor ("chaffare" in Chaucer's English meaning commerce), as well as its reduction of moral wheat to chaff, reads like a realization of the freest possible meaning of chaffering. Molly Bloom too is given to chaffering, and not only in the narrowly commercial sense. ("[A]nd the second pair of silkette stockings is laddered after one days wear I could have brought them back to Lewers this morning and kick up a row and made that one change them" [p. 702].) Even in talking to herself, she uses a sort of wrangling mode that presumes an other, someone complained of or to; while the Wife delivers a diatribe in the sense not only of a harangue but of an argument with an absent other (and for a large block of her Prologue impersonates her own opponent).[15] It is fitting, then, that with one or two exceptions Joyce's epithets for "Penelope" apply as well to the Wife: "perfectly sane full amoral fertilisable untrustworthy engaging shrewd limited prudent indifferent."[16] The Wife of Bath doesn't seem fertile—at least nowhere in her diatribe are children mentioned—and is not indifferent but struggles to establish her right to good things of the kind that would be called indifferent, that is, spiritually neutral and not worth fighting over, in the later history of the toleration argument. In fact the Wife has to contend for the sort of liberty that Molly Bloom seems to possess in full. Doesn't Bloom tell her in effect the words the Wife of Bath longs to hear, the words the one husband she loved told her, "Do as thee lust," Do as you like?

As noted before, many of the Canterbury pilgrims are portrayed as being superlative of their kind—so generic as it were that they become individual. A sort of special case of this paradox is presented by the Wife, possessing as she does all of the most reviled attributes of Woman, such as a lack of shame, but using them in a "shameless" struggle against the tradition that assigns her generic identity. From her opening polemic, where she turns the words of Paul against themselves and converts his prescriptions into grants of liberty, to her war with her fifth and dearest husband, the cleric, until he too gives her liberty, the Wife argues with a tradition of "auctoritee" that condemns her very battle as an expression of female license and perverse will. In a way the Wife is like a bear trapped in a net, the more entangled the more she struggles. Or like Horace's slave, taking the liberties of saturnalia and mocking his master, but confirming his subjection in so doing. Her struggle is not to be the mere incarnation of Woman that the tradition in the possession of her fifth husband declares her to be. With Molly Bloom there is nothing mere about incarnation, and in the fullness of her embodied life she seems to possess, as I've said, the autonomy the Wife of Bath craves.

Complicating our reading of the Wife of Bath is the sheer volume of her speech, both confirming the male caricature of Woman's excess and establishing that she is no mere product of the words of others but a voice in her own right. How *could* the Wife pay fealty to the very tradition that defines her as a satiric object? As we type others, so we resist being typed ourselves. "I cannot allow that my deeds, actions, words . . . should actualize nothing more than a certain type, that they should necessarily be predetermined by this typicality of mine."[17] In the Wife of Bath this "cannot," this moral necessity, takes the form of fighting off the words of men that she nevertheless "actualizes" and even uses for her own ends. The Wife, we know, derives from La Vieille of the *Romance of the Rose*, a voice of old experience, depraved, embittered, life-affirming, contradictory; and yet in waging war on the words of men, the Wife goes beyond her own original. Apparently Chaucer has transformed a satiric type in the direction of a person, an object in the direction of a subject. The Wife turns the Juvenalian tradition against itself, converting its very charges into weapons of her own. The Juvenalian Swift claimed to love individuals while hating lawyers, physicians, and mankind in general—another comment on the poverty of abstract definitions and categories. (Note that for all their weird egotism, the "authors" of A Tale of a Tub and "A Modest Proposal" are nameless, generic. *Ulysses* is stuffed with proper names.) So richly singular that she mocks her own definition as the eternal feminine, Molly Bloom seems to complete the series. The wealth of her inner speech alone means she "cannot" be a type of Woman and nothing more; in and of itself, the fact that her entire monologue is voiced only to herself seems to subvert the caricature of the gabbing woman.[18] It is as though Joyce turned the traditional objectification of Woman against itself in bringing Molly Bloom to life from within. And to turn the wheel yet another revolution, he presents the inner speech of this fully embodied being with an absence of editorial interference that makes her portrayal appear utterly objective. If Chaucer pretends not to be the author of the *Canterbury Tales*, Joyce's disappearance in the Penelope episode suggests that in the manner of the author of a polyphonic novel he has written himself out of the work and let his character speak, in effect renouncing the privilege of the authorial position.

What of Leopold Bloom, that "copy" of Odysseus who nevertheless seems a complete original? In some respects ordinary to the point of banality, Bloom is nevertheless so rich a character that he overfulfills the role of Everyman much as Molly does that of Woman. In the abundance of his being Bloom is like a coming-to-life of the satiric principle that "experience is bigger than any set of beliefs about it,"[19] since there is nothing about him that can't be turned to ridicule and perhaps nothing of importance to be said about him that can't be contradicted. Like his wife, at once "full" and "limited," who mocks our efforts to define her, Bloom is the creation of a satirist who knows the deficiency of schemes that "abstract from life."[20] He "ate with relish the inner organs of beasts and fowls" but in a vegetarian moment thinks of the "poor trembling calves" in the slaughterhouse (pp. 53, 163). He has a wondering, curious mind that stops musing and abridges its inquiry on the subject of his wife's infidelity. Even defining Bloom as a cuckold is no use. Here is a cuckold who vanquishes in defeat. While the cuckold is a starkly generic figure, the object of a thousand purely proverbial jokes in Shakespeare, Bloom is like none known—certainly not Charles Bovary, with his invincible ignorance, and not Chaucer's deceived husbands, either, although Chaucer's way of enriching such a skeletal form as the fabliau seems to prefigure Joyce's radical enrichment of the stock satiric figures of betrayed husband and unfaithful wife.[21] (Strangely, the cuckold of the Miller's Tale fails to conform to the type of the jealous husband assigned him in the tale itself. Not jealousy but a stunning lack of suspicion in fact distinguishes John.) Bloom's response to his plight, crystallized in moments when he shies from the sight or thought of Boylan as if both avoiding him and making way, is all at once a tactical prudence, an acceptance of something he can't change, a flight from knowledge, a surrender. His response is simply unique. It has nothing typical about it. If the parodist reproduces some original with a subversive difference—a technique Joyce knew well—Bloom explodes the very figure he exemplifies.[22]

Far from being a mock heroic work in the neoclassical manner, with Bloom a mock Odysseus, *Ulysses* undermines the hierarchy of styles on which the mock heroic is based. Where Pope ridicules bathos in a satiric treatise on "the art of sinking," Joyce so plays on bathos in reducing a hero to a modern middlebrow, and sins so comprehensively against Pope's maxims of style that we have to conclude he mocks the neoclassical order of values itself. "Above all," Pope states, "preserve a laudable prolixity; presenting the whole and every side at once of the image to view."[23] This satiric injunction becomes a virtual method in *Ulysses*, a masterpiece of prolixity whose hero is presented every which way, making it impossible for the reader to take up any single position toward him. In fact, just as it undercuts the hierarchy of styles, *Ulysses* baffles the neoclassical antithesis of satire and sympathy—the antithesis that made it possible for one critic to pronounce the two "absolutely incompatible."[24]

It is true that sympathy is ruled out for Swift's specimens of moral deformity, as satire is by the devout sympathy of Wordsworth. Nevertheless, as I've mentioned, the gothic Chaucer seems to have eluded the absolute of a later age, his Prioress, for example, being the object of a kind of love-leavened satire. The modulation of satire and sympathy that is one of the charms of Trollope reads like an extension of this authorial policy, with the novelist speaking for the general norms of courtesy as Chaucer does to the group that gave courtesy its name; and both in nuance. With Joyce we think not of the Prioress (mimic of courtly manners) but the Wife of Bath whose reckless display somehow wins us and establishes her humanity. As regards the hero of *Ulysses*, there can be no "balance" of satire and sympathy unless it be that each rises toward infinity. Bloom is subjected to such satiric exposure, particularly in Nighttown (where his trial and punishment burlesque the kind of liberal guilt that haunts Arthur Clennam), and yet evokes such fellow feeling from the reader that we can only give up on the antithesis between satire and sympathy and pronounce the man sui generis. In the mood of the carnivalesque, writes Bakhtin, praise and abuse, crowning and decrowning, are fused. Joyce seems to have caught this ambivalence in his portrayal of Bloom, turning him inside-out to the reader, crowning him with cuckold's horns, and converting his humiliations into a kind of victory. Now on the editorial page praise and abuse are not just distinct but absolutely incompatible. You praise good things and execrate bad things. It was Bakhtin's belief that when the carnival act of mockery loses the quality of ambivalence, it declines to the plainness of "naked journalism."[25]

The report of Mrs. Sinico's death is, in truth, naked—so bare as to be a mockery. The Deputy Coroner places the singular event of Mrs. Sinico's death in the class of accidents when it wasn't even accidental. Both Leopold and Molly Bloom are completely singular in spite of their membership in a class, his that of cuckold, hers unfaithful wife. It's as though the satiric insight of "A Painful Case," that schematic systems are incapable of containing the facts of experience (and this holds for Mr. Duffy's theories as well), became the principle of characterization in *Ulysses*. Now the Wife of Bath adopts "experience" as her battle cry and presents herself as one of those facts the clerical dogmas of men are incapable of containing. In this respect too *Ulysses* stands in the Chaucer tradition, or a Chaucer tradition. But if the Wife's speech is voiced (since as

Woman she insists on making herself public), it is above all the unvoiced speech of both of the Blooms that establishes their singularity. The transcription of inner speech authenticates both of them.

And this all the more because there is something overvoiced about a lot of the language in *Ulysses*, as though it were blown through some horn of Aeolus. In Chaucer's *House of Fame* Aeolus figures as the trumpeter of Fame, proclaiming the capricious judgments of that figure on the suits brought by all manner of human petitioners. Her decisions as diverse as the throng itself, Lady Fame awards infamy to some and renown to others on no principle and for no reason. Here, then, is another dramatization of the satiric insight that experience as given to us does not square with the schemes of reason. And the "diverse" sound of Aeolus' clarion (l. 1574) seems to echo in the satiric plenitude of languages in *Ulysses*, many with their oddity magnified. Aeolus of course figures in *Ulysses* more immediately as the god of wind presiding over the newspaper-office episode.[26] If Chaucer had lived in the twentieth century, he might well have viewed the press as an Aeolian horn blowing truth, rumor, and fable indistinguishably; while Joyce gives Aeolian treatment to Bloom not only by elevating him to an epic status he never sought (like some unassuming person, some Chaucer, in the temple of Fame) but by "de-faming" him, or showing him faults and all, at the same time.[27] That the *Telegraph* misprints Bloom's name as Boom, at once reducing and magnifying him to a blast of air, seems somehow right.[28]

As a tactic of political warfare, defamation in the everyday sense goes along with unmasking, itself a reduction of satiric action into a mode of violence. The unmasker violates you, not so much by getting inside your brain as by the falsity of his account of your brain. If only because the word "person" derives from that for "mask," it can be said that he strips you of personhood. In the totalitarian creeds that were making themselves known around the time of *Ulysses*'s publication, an obsession with unmasking produced not only systematic lying and savage caricature but the denial to many, notably Bloom's kinsmen the Jews, of the most elementary benefits of citizenship or civic personhood. Such a creed is like satire that has lost it mind. Joyce restores satire to its senses; and in exposing Bloom to the reader with a kind of anatomical effect never before seen in fiction, he does not discredit but actually establishes Bloom as a person.

*

In the last but one of the *Canterbury Tales* we are introduced to a wondrous crow able to "countrefete the speche of every man."[29] Reporting to Phoebus the infidelity of his wife, the bird is treated like the proverbial bearer of bad news—cast out, stripped of his power, and turned black. Where the poet masked the tales as a factual account to excuse the liberties of fiction, the Manciple's Tale, which echoes part of the apology of the General Prologue, seems to play up the risks of factual report. Joyce is Phoebus' crow, the counterfeiter of voices, in the fullness of his powers.

The stuff of the world in *Ulysses* is language in its Aeolian diversity, from the sentimentality of romantic fiction to the rant of political fanaticism—again recalling the *Canterbury Tales*, one a mock romance and one a recitation of the same anti-Semitic myth of ritual murder whose survival Bloom lays down to causes like popular superstition (p. 645). Joyce parodies styles by overvoicing them or rendering them with a kind of excessive perfection, by analogy with the surplus of being in Leopold and Molly Bloom that distinguishes them from the stylized figures of cuckolded husband and wayward wife. By holding up styles of language to the mirror of parody, the author both carries out and shatters the literary practice of mimesis.

Among the closer precursors of Molly is Emma Bovary, just as the prosecution of *Madame Bovary* prefigures the also unsuccessful suppression of *Ulysses*. For our purposes, though, what is more notable about that other art novel turned public scandal is the author's use of "style indirect libre" to record the speech and thoughts of his characters, a technique that produces an effect of satiric distancing even as it simulates objective report. ("How could she—she who was so intelligent!—have fooled herself one more time? Moreover, what deplorable mania had made her ruin her life by these constant sacrifices? She recalled . . . her dreams falling into the mud like wounded swallows.")[30] Given Flaubert's aim of depicting banalities and sentimental clichés with the utmost accuracy, report and satiric parody come more or less to the same thing in *Madame Bovary*. The same kind of stylistic rigor, the same ethos of keeping characters in character, was cited in the *Ulysses* decision in Joyce's favor.

In his decision admitting *Ulysses* into the United States, Judge Woolsey contends that its four-letter words, being in character for those who use them, are not gratuitous sprinklings of obscenity but evidences of the author's integrity and technical decorum.

> The words which are criticized as dirty are old Saxon words known to almost all men and, I venture, to many women, and are such words as would be naturally and habitually used, I believe, by the types of folks whose life, physical and mental, Joyce is seeking to describe. In respect of the recurrent emergence of the theme of sex in the minds of his characters, it must always be remembered that his locale was Celtic and his season [like Chaucer's] Spring.

In effect, Woolsey argues Joyce's propriety. In the *Romance of the Rose* Reason defends her use of colloquially anatomical language on the ground that it suits the word to the thing, a seriocomic claim that seems to launch the propriety argument. And with the quarrel over calling a thing by its rightful name in the *Romance of the Rose* we return to Chaucer.

It is not just that the *Romance of the Rose* supplied the model for the Wife of Bath herself. (If Joyce confounds the question of original and copy by making his "likeness" of Odysseus a perfect original, the Wife of Bath eclipses her own original and acts as though she had all the rights of independent existence.) Recall that after cataloging the Canterbury pilgrims Chaucer makes a prospective apology for the tales on the ground that he really had no choice but to report them in their "proper" words, that is, as they were told. Seeing that there is no event the *Canterbury Tales* records, Chaucer must really mean that someone like the Miller can only be expected to speak in character—to perform like the "goliardeys" he is. Preceded by another, closely similar disclaimer, the Miller's Tale itself overthrows the Knight's Tale, doing away with all cosmological machinery, reducing the courtly lady to a vital and not at all distant young wench, and removing events from ancient Athens to the here and now of Oxford.[31] Yet even as it turns the Knight's Tale upside down, the Miller's Tale in a sense preserves the hierarchy of styles, much as anticourtly speech in general presumes the existence of courtly models. The Miller's Tale confirms the code that decrees that from a churl like Robin the Miller only churlish things can be expected, and in fact it never pretends to be higher—grander, more stately, more philosophical—than the tale of the Knight. It is something like a carnival that turns the world upside down only to restore the world as it was in the end. So enduring was the hierarchy of styles that it remained the premise of neoclassical satire, only to be toppled by the age of revolution. In *Ulysses* the revolt is complete. Where *The Rape of the Lock* offers a ludicrously lowered version of a heroic original, *Ulysses* sounds mock heroic notes even as it explodes the moral stability of Pope's universe and throws into question the very distinction between the trivial and the great that his satire, and in fact much literary theory and practice, turns upon.[32]

But if Joyce demolishes the hierarchy of styles that survives even the subversions of the Miller's Tale, in another respect he is with Chaucer. Out of simple fabliaux, secondhand materials of all kinds, even preexisting characters Chaucer fashioned a work of the richest novelty. If the "now" of journalism negates the past, Chaucer found in tradition the very stuff of innovation and the means to speak to the present. Even the distinctly contemporary Miller's Tale sounds with echoes of the past in the sense that it answers a tale set in ancient Greece. Shot through with parodies of the Knight's Tale, the Miller's Tale possesses a "topicality"—an emphasis on location in time and space—that makes its point by contrast with a courtly romance set in the long ago and the far away. But not only does the Miller refer back to the preceding tale: more than this, the very genre his tale pertains to belongs to the preceding century. Before Chaucer was born the fabliau was obsolete.[33] It was not only a low genre but an extinct one that beckoned the poet at the height of his art. If the great fabliaux of the *Canterbury Tales* abolish the legendary or heroic past, and the reverence felt for it, in favor of the present moment, it was in fact by reviving a genre of the preceding century, a form whose possibilities might well have seemed exhausted, that Chaucer accomplished this effect. The present moment reverberates with the past. And so it is, of course, in *Ulysses*, a work whose topicality in exactly the sense of the Miller's Tale doesn't lose but somehow gains by virtue of the Homeric allusions seeded so cunningly in the text.

The present evokes the past: Joyce evokes Chaucer. A practically anti-thetical sense of time informs journalism as we know it—journalism being at this hour the public voice of the topical. For the consumer society not only holds the past to be dead and done with (mere "history") but likes to imagine itself free of the delusions that held humanity captive up to this hour. "History," says Stephen Dedalus, "is a nightmare from which I am trying to awake" (p. 34). The consumer society wakens every morning to a newspaper that proclaims the day a new one, yet "the news" is depressingly repetitive—a copy of a copy. The news is old even in its novelty. The Blooms are novel even in their antiquity. Haunted by predecessors, surrounded by echoes and double images, they are each one of a kind. *Ulysses* in this sense gives us journalism in reverse.

Moreover, it reclaims the freedom of speech that journalism institutional-izes. Seeing that Joyce professed little interest in Chaucer—though his library in 1920 contained Skeat's edition along with a book of excerpts from the *Canterbury Tales*, both stamped with his initials[34]—I am unable to account for the Chaucerian features of *Ulysses*, above all the reanimation of the Wife of Bath in Molly Bloom, except on the assumption that the author was led to these things by his understanding of satiric freedom itself. Persuaded that "experience is bigger than any set of beliefs about it," the satirist "demonstrates the infinite variety of what men do by showing the futility, not only of saying what they ought to do, but even of attempts to systematize or formulate a coherent scheme of what they do."[35] This the Wife of Bath freely translates into the argument that "God clepeth folk to hym in sondry wyse,"[36] and more particularly that in spite of Paul's emphasis on what we ought to do—remain unmarried—his words leave room for those like her with no such intention. And of course the Wife's ensign is "Experience." For two millennia, writes Elaine Pagels, "the majority of Christians . . . have chosen to maintain simultaneously Jesus' most extreme—even shocking—sayings, such as those prohibiting divorce and encouraging renunciation, together with others that modify their severity."[37] The Wife of Bath, with her satiric eye and her instinct for the cracks in the edifice of "auctoritee," makes the most of this discrepancy. And the remainder of her Prologue follows from her polemic with Paul, which is original with Chaucer. If, as I have proposed, freedom of speech rests on the insufficiency of our schemes and systems (in the sense that if they *were* sufficient, it would be heresy), the Wife brings out the very grounds of free speech with the greatest explicitness. In Leopold Bloom, at once hero and antihero, wise man and fool, we encounter a character larger than our predications about him. In Molly Bloom Joyce reimagines one who dramatizes the grounds of the freedom of speech for which *Ulysses* itself became a cause célèbre.

At some point, too, readers of *Ulysses* will disregard the "system" of correspondences they are cued to see as the key to this cryptic work. It's true that far from being a text where everything is held together by "organic filaments," *Ulysses* is held together inorganically, wired with allusions by a kind of Dedalian artifice. But the experience of reading it is something else again. (As the Wife of Bath would say, Experience knows it is not so.) As readers caught up in the wonders of this work, we necessarily overlook a lot of the intricacies of its wiring. And the work itself, for all of the excessive complication of its "system," induces this effect. "The flow of material wars against a technology which, however determined, is inadequate to the task of controlling the material."[38] This discordance may reflect a crisis of the modern moment; it also reflects a tradition of satiric freedom.

Ulysses seems in fact to tap the very source of satiric energy, energy free in the sense that it is independent of the genres it animates, notably comedy, tragedy, and the novel itself. Everyone, I imagine, feels the inadequacy of calling this work which resembles nothing but itself a "novel." According to Northrop Frye, *Ulysses* is a "complete prose epic" made up equally of novel, romance, confession, and anatomy (or Menippea)[39]—which is also to say, however, that it defies classification and constitutes a category in its own right. I have suggested that the works of Dickens, which resemble nothing so much as one another, compose a virtual genre unto themselves; similarly those of Austen. Joyce in effect made a genre of a single work. And being sui generis, literally one of a kind, it is in harmony with its own hero and heroine.

CHAPTER 9

Orwell: The Return to Origins

The Paris section of Orwell's first book, which bears an ironic epigraph from Chaucer, resembles a *Canterbury Tales* stripped down to the fabliaux. Like Chaucer, Orwell the *plongeur* seems the last and least of a company ordered by rank:

> Our staff, amounting to about a hundred and ten, had their prestige graded as accurately as that of soldiers, and a cook or waiter was as much above a *plongeur* as a captain above a private. Highest of all came the manager, who could sack anybody, even the cooks,[1]

who are dirty like the Canterbury cook. Orwell's account of life at the bottom is laced with tales of trickery, of taking and mistaking, but they are tales imputed to others, for like Chaucer the author subordinates himself to more colorful characters. An air of wicked levity, recalling the fabliau, invigorates an otherwise depressing report. As in the fabliau, the cast of this social underworld seem to live finally by their wit. The eye for detail and the logistical sense of the Chaucerian fabliau—the breakdown of action into its elements of what, why, where, when, how—are also at work in *Down and Out in Paris and London*.

In the fabliau showing cheats and cuckolds for what they really are, the satiric project of exposure is at its plainest. The exposure of idiocy is Swift's declared intention in the *Tale of a Tub*. In Engels's *Condition of the Working Class in England*, which brings to light denied realities and unmasks the English bourgeois who "tries to hide his selfish greed in the most hypocritical manner"[2] (the phrasing is traditional), exposure has turned to exposé. Orwell's investigations of poverty and descents into the depths, literal descent in *The Road to Wigan Pier*, are in the same spirit of documentation, although as a literary man Orwell remains within a satiric tradition that cannot be reduced to a set of political theses or "laws." The first of the Canterbury fabliaux is already impossible to slot politically, its speech too broad and satire too strong to conform to familiar political categories.[3] That quality shows itself in Orwell's first book and reaches full intensity in his last.

*

In his last and most important book, Orwell brought to completion his work as a journalist by getting down to satire.[4] In a way he perhaps didn't envision, *Nineteen Eighty-four* also produced in some circles one of the effects of satire: scandal. To some of the left Orwell is a traitor to the cause, an instigator of the cold warriors of Washington, his most celebrated work deriving its power from a reactionary fantasy. Smears aside, it is not easy to label Orwell politically. Out of the satiric tradition come the perversity and futility arguments of right and left, still inflected with scorn and ridicule. (Revolution is doomed to catastrophe; it is no use resisting the decree of history.) Orwell, adopting some conservative and some progressive positions, prizes above all freedom of speech, whose exercise took him to the extremity of satire. The satiric potential that modern political dogmas lock up, each in its own manner, Orwell taps into directly. His affinity is accordingly less with a political camp than with a satiric line.

A Tory anarchist, he called himself—and Swift.[5] That each lashed the intellectual, that the comments of both on the corruption of the English tongue are in the tradition of Lucian's ridicule of linguistic pretension, that each asks us to "credit the inconceivable"—Orwell in *Nineteen Eighty-four*, Swift in "A Modest Proposal"—these resemblances only begin to mark the affinity between the two.[6] In fact Orwell wrote about both Swift and his satiric kinsmen Smollett and Dickens with the warmth that distinguishes his best essays, and while he never discussed Joyce at any length, he was strongly impressed with *Ulysses* in spite of the author's aestheticism and seeming removal from politics, and put Joyce along with Swift, Dickens, and a few others on his list of best-loved authors.[7] Swift, Smollett, Dickens, even Joyce, perhaps: the most extravagant satirists in English are remembered in depth in Orwell's prose, in the way the master of a genre might tap into the sources and spirit of the genre itself. Not only did Orwell possess this kind of memory, he exposed the kind of counterfeit language—"generic," it might be called—that is the product of the assault on memory. Under the reign of the Party in Oceania the richness of a language informed by tradition gives way to the automatism of formula. In "Politics and the English Language" an example of verbal deformity is judged against the prose of the King James Bible (which lends resonance in turn to Dickens). Although not in the strict sense a conservative or for that matter a religious man, Orwell is convinced that without a living sense of tradition the life goes out of language as well.

Of the two Chaucer lines Orwell evidently belongs to the second—
"Politics and the English Language" answering the Swiftian "Art of Canting."
So clearly do Orwell's sympathies lie with the line of Swift rather than the more
decorous Addisonians, about whom he has little to say, that one might classify
him a Swiftian too and leave it at that but for two facts: first, that authors of
real magnitude are unlikely to fit any scheme that gets too schematic (Swift
by his own description was a Tory in Church and a Whig in politics);[8] second,
the pretensions of systems and schemes are a traditional target of satire in their
own right. Orwell himself, moreover, seems to possess something of the quality
of embarrassing dogmas and doctrines that satire does.[9] A thorn to his fellow
intellectuals, a scandal to the orthodox, Orwell has a way of confounding our
classifications. Like Leopold Bloom, who fascinated him, Orwell politically
speaking was a Jew whose homeland lay somewhere in the imagination. The
man doesn't fit preexisting categories of any kind, which is probably why he's
been called so many things. Irving Howe once called him a revolutionary with
a conservative streak.[10]

The same issues Orwell had been drawing attention to in his journalism
are presented with the starkest intensity in *Nineteen Eighty-four*, as though satire
finished what journalism began. Like Dickens, then, Orwell took the journey
from reportage to satire; like Swift in "A Modest Proposal" he reached the
extremity of satire as he neared the end of his work. In that journalism itself
begins in satire, though, Orwell's journey was also a return to origins. Of the
varieties of satire, Orwell chose in *Nineteen Eighty-four* the freest in its handling
of ideas and the best adapted to the subversion of those hardened ideas we
call ideologies—the Menippea; and as Bakhtin has noted, Menippean satire is
journalistic in spirit:

> [The Menippea] is, in its own way, the "journalistic" genre of antiquity,
> acutely echoing the ideological issues of the day. . . . A journalistic quality,
> the spirit of publicistic writing or of the feuilleton, a pointed interest in
> the topics of the day are characteristic to a greater or lesser extent of all
> representatives of the menippea,[11]

among them *Nineteen Eighty-four*. So it is that any number of the most striking
features of *Nineteen Eighty-four* reflect those of the genre itself—outrageous paradoxes like "War is peace" attesting the Menippea's love of "sharp contrasts and
oxymoronic combinations";[12] the interpolation of "The Book," the Menippea's
play with inserted genres; the final evocation of a man on the threshold of
execution (a setting with strong echoes of both Dostoevsky and Boethius),

the Menippean feeling for threshold locations like the gates of heaven and the doors of death; the refrain "We are the dead,"[13] the Menippean mixing of the living and the dead; indeed, the what-if premise of the whole, the Menippean passion for experiment. In stretching our sense of the believable, *Nineteen Eighty-four* stands in the same tradition as *Gulliver's Travels*, itself strongly engaged with the issues of the day. The Menippean Chaucer for his part likes to set up lectures by a figure overstocked with wisdom—it may be a magical crone, a rooster, a personification like Prudence.[14] In the Knight's Tale this becomes Theseus rationalizing the behavior of the gods, and overwhelming Emily's resistance to marriage as he once defeated the queen of the Amazons, by means of a pompous philosophical harangue (a discourse subversively echoed in Nicholas's information about the heavens in the Miller's Tale). O'Brien's tutelage of Winston Smith, even for that matter his lack of human attributes, reflects this literary motif. O'Brien baring his own fraud as no human being really would calls up the "black journalism" of Lucian where the wise bare their own folly.[15] "You are a flaw in the pattern," Smith is informed by his preceptor.[16] In subjecting totalitarianism to satire—which laughs at systems and dogmas as well as their makers, likes to bring up "inconvenient data,"[17] and indulges an excess that mocks the pretensions of design—Orwell answers the great threat to freedom of speech by getting down close to the root of free speech itself. Perhaps the most topical novel of its time, *Nineteen Eighty-four* is informed by the ancient spirit of the Menippea.

In *Homage to Catalonia*, a work with a rich satiric undertone (and critical of the lies of journalists), Orwell fondly recalls what it was like to be one of

> tens of thousands of people, mainly though not entirely of working-class origin, all living at the same level and mingling on terms of equality. In theory it was perfect equality, and even in practice it was not far from it. . . . Many of the normal motives of civilized life—snobbishness, money-grubbing, fear of the boss, etc.—had simply ceased to exist.[18]

We are reminded of the satiric equality of the dead in Lucian: in death "you see how the millionaires and the pashas and the dictators have been cut down to size and look just like everybody else." This from *Dialogues of the Dead*, where a philosopher asks Menippus himself, "How about getting rid of that independence, frank speaking, cheery resignation, high-mindedness, and mockery?"[19] Just these qualities—in which Bakhtin, the great student of the Menippean tradition, locates the spirit of free speech[20]—illumine *Homage to Catalonia*. In the same work we encounter a dog endowed with an almost human consciousness, as though the equality of souls extended even beyond humanity.

> Every militia column had at least one dog attached to it as a mascot. One wretched brute that marched with us had P.O.U.M. branded on it in huge letters and slunk along as though conscious that there was something wrong with its appearance.[21]

We seem to be reading Dickens, possibly with some satire *of* Dickens admixed. The pages of Orwell are populous with the shades of his predecessors.

We have no ready term for the sort of memory at work in the evocation of literary precedents possibly unknown, some of them, to the author himself. "Unconscious recall" might seem right, except that it's overloaded with psychological connotations and psychology itself has usurped the satiric project of holding up the mirror to our own nature and curing disease and delusion.[22] "Genre memory" is more apt.[23] In making the case that Dostoevsky understood the genre of Menippean satire right down to its roots, Bakhtin instances a strange story entitled "Bobok." From its narrator "who is despised by everyone and who himself despises everyone" to its imagery of eating, drinking, and gambling in the face of death to its device of discarding shame and telling all, "Bobok" echoes in the most haunting way the performance of Chaucer's Pardoner, which neither Dostoevsky nor Bakhtin may ever have read.[24] Orwell's evocation of the history of the genre is as telling as that. Like the Pardoner himself—a re-creation of yet another character—there is in this kind of recall something deeper than a common allusion. It is as if the recovery of the past frustrated within *Nineteen Eighty-four*, with Winston Smith's failure to put together his own past or to make anything of an incriminating photograph, were richly accomplished at another level. Like Joyce, who elicits the present moment by means of an ancient archetype; like Chaucer using the dead genre of the fabliau to create a vivid feeling of topical immediacy (and *Down and Out in Paris and London* is interleaved with tales of this kind), Orwell delves into the past to bring out the present. It is ironic that satire, with its grounding in the past, should underwrite journalism that now plays havoc with the sense of the past itself.

The life of perhaps every society features rites of renewal, returns to the beginnings of things. Bakhtin's view seems to be that a Dostoevsky renews his genre by tapping its original spirit and potential. In *Nineteen Eighty-four* it is as though the author sought to renew journalism by putting it back in touch with satire, which it originally was. Reminiscent of Dostoevsky, himself a sometimes journalist, the heightened vision of *Nineteen Eighty-four* bears witness to a power much older than the newspaper. Strangely, it was by entering into the spirit of an ancient genre that Orwell was able to realize so well the nature of totalitarianism, a system of government marking a radical departure from the past. It is not only that in Oceania as in the USSR the ruling ideology demands the creation and execution of enemies, so that Winston Smith's attempt to resist the design that contains him is doomed—his efforts at revolt having been superintended and even possibly incited by the state. (It is as though not only Joyce but Orwell radicalized the Wife of Bath's struggle against the "auctoritee" that defines her.) With the fall of East European despotisms one after the other a few years ago, it became clear that Orwell was more right in his depiction of totalitarianism than we were ever really prepared to recognize. Out of his own genius for disenchantment and his sense of the historical sources of journalism Orwell actually grasped the nature of the thing in *Nineteen Eighty-four*. What had seemed to some readers the lurid imaginings of a sick mind, or just shock effects, turned out to be an all-too-accurate vision of life in a prison-camp society. Are the rites of worship in *Nineteen Eighty-four* so far beyond the forced adulation of Ceaucescu? Is Orwell's depiction of a society totally penetrated by the secret police belied by the Stasi of East Germany? Is the pall of foulness that hangs over life in Oceania an exaggeration next to the hideous pollution of earth and air in Poland? An ancient genre brings out the nature of a monstrous novelty of the twentieth century. If totalitarianism is in fact driven by monologic—by ever more extreme iterations of a single brute idea—then perhaps it stands to reason that Orwell's exposé of this new terror should be informed by the tradition of the *dia*logic imagination.[25]

Perhaps the most eminent political philosopher of our age is at one with Orwell in *Nineteen Eighty-four*. The great theme of Isaiah Berlin's thought is the utopian fallacy—the fatal lure of some scientific society in which all questions receive their final solution and in whose name no human sacrifice is unjustified. For Berlin in turn, the most trenchant critic of the utopian fallacy may be Alexander Herzen, the freethinker who in exile from Russia edited the dissident journal *The Bell*.

> If progress is the goal [writes Herzen], for whom are we working? Who is this Moloch who, as the toilers approach him, instead of rewarding them, draws back; and as a consolation to the exhausted and doomed multitudes, shouting "morituri te salutant," can only give the . . . mocking answer that after their death all will be beautiful on earth,[26]

Oceania being a vision of this posthumous paradise, with Moloch become Big Brother. The traditional satiric insight that the attempt "to create Progress . . .

produces its opposite" is raised to the last pitch of irony. "The brave new world [becomes] a living hell."[27] Now as Berlin emphasizes throughout his writings and in fact in the work from which this outcry by Herzen is quoted, the corrective of the utopian delusion is simply the understanding that conflicts over ends rather than means are not resolvable, that there is no and can be no final solution to human questions. "If some ends recognised as fully human are at the same time ultimate and mutually incompatible, then the idea of a golden age, a perfect society compounded of a synthesis of all the correct solutions to all the central problems of human life, is shown to be incoherent in principle."[28] Values and visions clash: do we not encounter this principle in a kind of politically uncodified form in the *Canterbury Tales*, which impress us more with their manyness than their unity, more by their clashes and ironic echoing than their resolutions, and whose "dialogic" quality of resonant discord somehow survives not only the final tale but even the poet's own retraction?

*

Like many before him, Orwell was convinced of the linkage between the condition of language and that of the polity. In "Politics and the English Language" as in *Nineteen Eighty-four* the corruption of the word is shown as both cause and effect of the decay of political freedom. But to what original should a now corrupted language be restored? Both Wordsworth and Byron, persuaded of the link between bad style and public ills, sought to purify and renovate verse, except that the vicious style that Byron wanted to do away with was Wordsworth's. In a section of his *Essay* devoted to abuses of words, Locke employs a modest style in character with his desire to lower political passions and cure distempers of thought; yet Swift shows the modest style itself to be a distemper of thought. No uncontested principles for the proper use of language exist.

All the same, in "Politics and the English Language" Orwell recommends a few simple checks for writers to perform to make sure their words don't amount to so much gas like the examples of prose infamized in the essay. His own writing isn't so simple. Much as the minimalism of Hemingway (at one time a reporter) implies a sweeping rejection of Victorian narration—its prolixity, its sentiment, its reputed intellectual dishonesty—so Orwell seems to say more by saying less. And it is his tie with the satiric tradition of Swift, a tradition that includes the Victorian Dickens, that gives his word much of its ironic resonance. No set of rules including his own makes Orwell's prose what it is. In all probability something written by his rules would turn out generic, a bare shell of words that scores well on a readability scale but lacks the quality of evocation. Nor do his rules even guarantee honesty, seeing that lies can be uttered in lean prose as well as the opposite. Orwell's rules aren't worth much. As a prescription for simplicity, in fact, they bear an awkward resemblance to the Oceanic policy of cutting down language to the very minimum in the interest of reducing thought. The best of the rules is a reminder of Blake's inverted commandments. It says break any of the others "sooner than say anything outright barbarous."[29] (In a sense, Orwell does break his rules by using as a touchstone the King James Bible instead of some simplified edition.) This last, saving proviso is in the spirit of satiric ridicule of mechanical systems, which is also to say that Orwell writes in the tradition of the satirist satirized. Without such critical turns, satire might devolve into one of the dogmas it sought to expose.[30]

Chaucer for his part satirizes himself as well as his objects in the *Canterbury Tales*. Part of this fooling strategy, as we know, is the pretense of reporting the words of the pilgrims—pilgrims "mingling on terms of equality," with the same chance to speak—as though they weren't his own creation in the first place. But it may be apt here, in closing, to reconsider Chaucer's disclaimer of poetic authority. An essay on Bakhtin's dislike of ready-made ideas—the equivalent of Orwell's dislike of ready-made phrases in "Politics and the English Language"—takes note of his denial "that the world is adequately and in principle exhaustively describable in terms of a set of norms and rules."[31] Maybe Chaucer waived his poetic authority not just to win the audience's indulgence of his fiction (all the world loves humility) but because he really didn't want to become an "auctor," a source of norms, one whose example possesses the force of a rule. Maybe his posture as one of no authority was more than a pose after all—was a genuinely Socratic act. Of *Homage to Catalonia* Lionel Trilling wrote, "It is a very modest book—it seems to say the least that can be said on a subject of great magnitude."[32] Perhaps more suggestively than anything else, this Socratic quality, present in much of his work, places our greatest quasi journalist in the tradition of Chaucer. Both he and Chaucer stand in the satiric tradition, going back to Socrates, of the "truly free investigation of the world."[33]

Afterword

Through the writings of the great historian of ideas Isaiah Berlin runs a single theme like a scarlet thread: not even in theory can all interpretations of the good be harmonized. Our ends are many, not one; consistency eludes us. This principle, however, was already known to satire (itself a mix of things) and, among the satirists, especially well understood by Chaucer. Courtly love is taken seriously in the Knight's Tale only to be ridiculed by the Miller. The ethos of every man for himself "seems sensible in 'The Reeve's Tale,' but mean in the selfless world of the Franklin." The Wife of Bath, a kind of standard-bearer of inconsistency, uses patristic arguments to defend her own interests.[1] What is more, the very form of the *Canterbury Tales* is splintered between the General Prologue and the Tales per se, the former arising from estates satire with its hierarchical orderings, the latter with ties to the more disorderly Menippean tradition. As I have surmised, the reason Joyce shows a likeness to Chaucer isn't that he wanted to pay homage to him but that Chaucer grasped so well the principle of plenitude that was Joyce's too—Berlin lists Joyce among his foxes, or pluralists—and that the Wife of Bath, precursor of Molly Bloom, brings to life and defends. Reading the *Canterbury Tales*, reading *Ulysses*, we sense the root meaning of satire itself: a plenty. It is especially ironic, then, that satire, with its irreducible richness and its resistance to formula, should have been reduced in the modern age to a source of formula itself—much as the satiric exposure of private life was mechanically reproduced in journalism by the end of the nineteenth century.

Perhaps the satiric tradition can be imagined as so much capital underwriting the practice of journalism. The Victorians some say lived off their moral inheritance, which may or may not imply it was used up. Consumer society a century later, true to its name and more radical than its Victorian forebear, liquidates cultural capital, not only converting it into a generic product but undoing the memory of such wealth to begin with. The process of decapitalization may have begun, however, with the reduction of satire to the stuff of straight political doctrine, and the satiric exposure of idiocy and delusion to the practice of laying bare the minds and schemes of ideological enemies. Who can tell how much the drive to strip bare—once a satiric liberty, now a political commonplace, a commercial formula, in fact a pretense in its own right—has contributed to the reign of "simplification and brutality"[2] in our time? Enacted with a realism that is itself brutal, the satiric cure becomes a political purge, the penetration of appearances an obsession with hidden enemies, the caricature a smear. At times satire comes to life for the worse, "as when the mirror is abandoned for the scourge, pen for the sword, and rapier wit yields to a true 'envenom'd point,'"[3] or when the surgical execution that is Dryden's image of satire yields to the guillotine, or the drive to "clear the world at once from folly, vanity, and affectation"[4] inspires the proclamation of Year One.

The critic cited just above, Gerald Bruns, questions the once influential view of satire as an expression of superior sanity and wonders if the genre is instead "not intrinsically rational" at all, merely "a certain way of speaking to be adopted by any ideology whatever," an instrument available for different uses.[5] My sense is that while satire doesn't equate with moral reason, neither does it lend itself to different interests so much as it is captured by them—its excess appropriated, its liberty reined in. But that it ends up in various hands seems true enough. The abundance of the satiric tradition is such that it powers not only both Marxist and conservative arguments but even, as I have proposed, the political economy that Marx contradicted and that journalism conveys in popular form to this day.

Perhaps the neutrality ascribed to satire by Gerald Bruns shows itself as well in a kind of indifference to literary form. Not so much a form as a potential tapped by different forms, satire is worked in the direction of comedy in the *Canterbury Tales* (with its projected reconciliation of parties at a final feast) and into tragedy in *Hamlet*, its hero at once mirror and scourge, wit and swordsman.[6] *Gulliver's Travels* strikes us as comic in a sort of tragic way, as though it made use of a power anterior to genre itself. Dickens, a comic master, deepens his most satiric work with overtones of *King Lear*. Possibly it is the very "informality" of satire that recommends it so particularly to the least formally specified of all literary genres, the novel, to begin with. Now it is Bakhtin's belief that the novel, with its orchestration of languages, does the fullest justice to the truth that human experience "is always richer, more fundamental and most importantly *too contradictory and heteroglot* to be fit into a high and straightforward genre [sic]."[7] But this, as we know, is also a premise of satire, and in fact Bakhtin is recurrently drawn to satire, whether in the form of the fabliau or the Menippea, in his reflections on the novel. (Additionally, Bakhtin's main predications about the novel, of which the cited statement is representative, hold true of Chaucer in his capacity as satirist.)[8] If the ablest American interpreter of Bakhtin emphasizes the danger of theory and the primacy of the prosaic, just these themes—the deceptions of theory and the value of "living an ordinary life in an everyday world"—figure strongly in the great satirist, Lucian.[9] I suggest that satire realizes freedom of speech as Bakhtin claims of the novel. Presumably it is Bakhtin's opposition to the cult of Stalin as epic hero, and to the suppression of critical speech and thought that accompanied it, that underlies his contrast between epic and novel, which is all in the novel's favor. Epic, a finished genre, presents a closed world; the novel opens the world by enabling free and full investigation. Such is Bakhtin's esteem for the principle of open possibility that to pursue his line of thinking is to ask how a story can be told that isn't predetermined and how to depict an event that need never have happened at all.[10] In English literature, as it happens, the work that most conspicuously fulfills these requirements isn't a novel but a satire, or if you will an ironized epic, Byron's *Don Juan*. The narrative of *Don Juan* is open in the double sense that it was composed practically without a design (and overflows the original design of twelve cantos) and registers events that may or may not take on significance, depending on how things unfold.[11] But what is Byron after in this notably heteroglot and contradictory work? Freedom of speech. "Why, Man, the soul of such writing is its license."

And satire is well fitted to be the carrier of such freedom. If the novel in Bakhtin's view is unbound by the presumptions of other genres (thus constituting a sort of supergenre), the freedom of satire is such that it overflows every generic boundary and its power such that it animates different genres in the first place. The satiric principle works in romance, in comedy, in tragedy—that the fate of the tragic hero cannot be squared with reason testifies to a satiric view of schemes and systems—in the most seminal of novels, *Don Quixote. Ulysses*, at the summit of the satiric tradition in English, is like Bloom himself in one respect: both are sui generis. The supreme formalization of satire in English literature, on the other hand, may be "The Vanity of Human Wishes," which thus contains an element of vanity itself. Surely it was the great potential of the satiric word—a power that flows through literature—that attracted the authors of modern polemic to satire in the age of revolution not long after Johnson's death, when his own perception of the futility of human ambitions was reduced to a generic political thesis.

As I have proposed, since the time of the French Revolution political creeds have put the power of satire to work, constructing doctrines and dogmas from satiric sources. From the satiric intuition that reality dashes our schemes and pretenses conservatism takes possibly its core thesis—that schematic plans for the construction of society are bound to fail—as does the left its conviction that the plots and schemes of secret enemies, as well as the less conscious ingenuities of the opponents of progress, that is, the ideology in which they mask reality even from themselves, are destined for defeat. Both doctrines owe some of their power to the appropriation of a literary force so fundamental it fires different genres; both add an aspect of philosophical depth to rhetorical show, and both take their spark from the French Revolution. In response to the Revolution, satiric insights like Adam Smith's into "systems . . . which act contrary to the very end which they propose"[12] evolved into the argument that seizing liberty produces only slavery. (Adam Smith has a pronounced satiric streak of his own, his insight into folly and knavery as acute as Swift's or Pope's. That he is less doctrinaire than later exponents of what came to be called laissez-faire probably reflects his greater proximity to the satiric tradition, a tradition that confounds the definitions of critics and ridicules formula itself.) What with its criticism of the futile and self-deluded, and yet for all that dangerous, attempt to evade objective reality, conservatism in effect claims satire for its own. In time the left would come to speak of the ideology of its opponents in like terms, as a delusion at once vain and dangerous, just as it would invert Adam Smith's thesis in asserting that capitalism itself merely prepares its own downfall. Though parading as science, Marxism draws on satire. Arguments like "resisting History's decree is self-defeating" not only have the ring of satiric derision, they amount to paraphrase of an insight into human futility so traditional to satire that it has been called its very plot.[13] Satire has hardened into creed. Out of the freedom of satire comes the standardization of thought, out of its plenitude, the materials of mental narrowness. If Dickens's characters, like William Dorrit, get locked into fictions of their own creation, if their speech becomes formulaic (as if they had lost the freedom in which their fictions originate), our formulas come to us ready-made, fashioned largely of the stuff of satire.

Among the high and straightforward genres too narrow for the novel (in Bakhtin's view) would be tragedy. Exemplary among tragedies is *Oedipus the King*. And bearing out the principle that satire is a fuel of genres rather than a genre in its own right, this work itself seems to derive power from satiric sources. Not only are the cure of vice and the exposure of hypocrisy and delusion, so familiar to us in the later history of satire, enacted here with the highest seriousness, but the primal satiric act of indicting or cursing one in the name of many is evoked with almost excessive clarity. The freedom of speech I have situated in the satiric tradition is dramatized in *Oedipus*, too, with the hero demanding to be told all, and others, sensing or knowing that all is too much, attempting to brake the process. "Who among you knows the murderer / by whose hand Laius, son of Labdacus, / died—I command him to tell everything / to me." "Would you provoke me into speaking?" (Teiresias). "I have spoken far too much" (Jocasta). "Jocasta, I will tell you the whole truth." "O God, I am on the brink of frightful speech" (Herdsman). Here then is "the provocation of the word by the word"[14] in its starkest and most tragic aspect. Now in reflecting on the genealogy of the conservative argument that actions backfire, Albert O. Hirschman speculates that some of its power may lie in a recall of Greek legend. "Man undertakes an action and is successful at first, but success leads to arrogance and, in due course, to setback, defeat, disaster."[15] The reduction of the enigma of *Oedipus* to a pat thesis, and the drama of speech to the debating tactics cataloged by Hirschman (but by no means confined to conservatives), the reduction of a delusion both profound and treacherous to a common political ailment—let this illustrate the sacrifice of satiric freedom in the formulas of modern polemic.

*

With modernity goes what some call the rationalization of the world, a process comprehending the invalidation of myth and magic, the more efficient adaptation of means to ends, and the expansion of technical control over wider regions of life. Jeremy Bentham campaigning against a gothic past in the name of efficiency, clarity, and the general good provides a symbol of the rationalization of the world.

Let me propose that one like Bentham who bares the truth of things with a show of devastating effect—who claims a kind of objective insight that explodes deceit and delusion—rationalizes the power of satire. In satire per se is much that is *un*rationalized: an excess of information (as in Joyce), of anger (in the Juvenalian tradition), of language itself (in Rabelais), of targets (in Swift). Some of this excess, moreover, survives the "rationalization" of satire. Doesn't the term itself, after all, hint at a mere show of reason, a papering-over of some underlying embarrassment? Bentham himself, whose thought once supplied John Stuart Mill with a rational "creed,"[16] still rails and ridicules like a satirist in his *Book of Fallacies*. Ceaselessly repeated exposés in the mass media, the ideologue's show of knowing so much more than his adversaries that, like Bentham penetrating the schemes of the wicked, he can see through their very brains—these are among the vestiges of satiric excess.

The freedom of satire, however, is unlikely to survive translation into generic arguments or indeed the journalism that conveys them to the public.[17]

Though Jane Austen has been read as a purveyor of the clichés of conser-vatism,[18] there remains in her satire something too knifelike to be quite civil, too oblique to conform to her own ideal of plainspokenness, too original to be doctrinaire. Such excess is that much more pronounced in Swift. By the end of *Gulliver's Travels*, indeed, doctrine has been overpowered by satire and the work appears to leave the category of the didactic altogether. Overthrown by a mutinous crew, Gulliver has found what seems like refuge in the land of the horses, noble animals who make European society seem bestial by contrast. Yet these masters of themselves, these paragons of Reason who meet death with equanimity, conceive the totally irrational fear that Gulliver will foment a revolt of their slaves (irrational if only because Gulliver, the victim of mutiny, is the last person imaginable to stage a mutiny). So immoderately do the horses hate their Yahoos that like perfect totalitarians they debate whether to exterminate or just sterilize them—that is, to eliminate them at once or over time.[19]

What exactly to make of this spectacle of reason gone mad is hard to know. Can we say that Swift turns against his own preoccupation with "asepsis"—against that in him that says "the problem is one of purging—of getting the germ out and keeping it out"?[20] Possibly. By the conclusion of *Gulliver's Travels*, when the hero camps in his stable to get away from his detested family, the worship of equine wisdom is in any case surely in doubt. Swift's satire veers sharply, as though the liberty of his pen, as he calls it in the Preface to *A Tale of a Tub*, could not conform itself after all to the terms of a one-dimensional argument. If the horses are an ideal commonwealth, hadn't he once linked utopias with things like the philosopher's stone, all of them fumes of the brain?[21] Maybe it was some counsel of satiric wisdom that induced Swift to make Gulliver fit so badly into the horses's scheme of classification (being neither a Yahoo nor one of them) and make the horses, in their own estimation the perfection of Nature, plot like paranoids to get rid of him. Recalling the dizzying turns of More's *Utopia*, the riddles Swift leaves us with seem to reflect the paradox of the seriocomic as such. Satire has a trick of returning on itself. The extremity of Swift's indictment of Europe produces a certain turning of the tables on the Houyhnhnms themselves; the vitriol of antifeminism elicits the vitality of the Wife of Bath; the most impoverished of satiric figures, the cuckold and the straying wife, bring forth the satiric riches of Joyce. Originating in the indictment and the curse, satire in Joyce's hands becomes affirmation.

Without the power to turn back on itself in this way, satire would lose a saving element of free play. With the translation of satire into straight invective (another liquidation of cultural wealth), the freedom of theoriginal is in fact lost and satire becomes the equivalent of an act of force. Not Swift but the totalitarians are really possessed by the myth of asepsis—the Nazis in their drive to disinfect the Reich of the Jews, the Stalinists in their enthusiasm for the purge. When Gulliver eulogizes a society with none of the depravity of Europe, no pride, no vanity, no vice of any kind, does anyone suppose the author dreams of actually clearing London of its entire population—the only way to achieve such an aseptic state—as was done in our own time in the city of Phnom Penh? Swift has no program for getting rid of undesirables, and in his most perfect satire savages one—an enumerated benefit of the Modest Proposal being the thinning of the population of Catholics. If he plays with fire in his satire, nevertheless it *is* play. In his very indignation is a current of laughter, a presence of Rabelais. Such qualifications serve to distinguish satire from doctrinaire argument and invective.

Even Jane Austen, deemed by one well-informed reader a straight conservative, proves hard to define or "rationalize" politically. How can Jane Austen be presenting a straight Burkean view of the world as an unbroken chain of the generations when her great heroines, Elizabeth Bennet, Emma Woodhouse, Fanny Price, are all virtual orphans? I am reminded here of the insufficiency of my own design, since in endowing such orphan figures so richly with exceptionality—in realizing the miracle of moral consciousness amid such a general lack of mind—Austen bears comparison with a member of the opposite satiric line, Dickens. In contrast with the doctrines and dogmas that exploit the power of satire, real satiric vision and power are unlikely to show all things in exactly one way.

The very figure of the one-eyed is the cyclops; and the Cyclops episode of *Ulysses* takes us inside the language world of political fanaticism. (Joyce's name for the narrator of the episode was Thersites, after the archsatirist of *Troilus and Cressida*.) In and of itself, the double vision induced by *Ulysses* seems a reflection on such a mentality. If the primal satiric act bonds the group against some reviled other, Joyce in *Ulysses* takes nation building to a higher level, "summon[ing] into being a society capable of reading and enjoying" his own book.[22] A less visionary worker for the reconstruction of society was the great Russian expatriate Herzen, whose writings are lit up with satiric power. Giving play to a lashing wit and mocking those "accustomed to a moral at the end of the fable, to systematic formulae, to classification, to binding, abstract prescriptions,"[23] Herzen exposes the fanatic's dream of a utopia at the end of history that demands the slaughter of multitudes and the extinction of liberty. Herzen saw himself "as an expert 'unmasker' of appearances and conventions, and dramatised himself as a devastating discoverer of their social and moral core."[24] Such exhibitions of power, however, are also staged by ideologues. Marx too was acclaimed a devastating discoverer, one who smashed falsehood that truth could at last be revealed; and totalitarianism itself claims the key to a reality hidden behind the world of appearances.[25] The suspension of written law that Hannah Arendt remarked in the totalitarian state and Orwell made a feature of Oceania—can this be taken as a kind of malign application of satire's contempt for schematic rules and constructs?[26]

As an example of the reduction of satire to ideology, consider the case of one of the most influential ever composed, a superb Menippea translated by Chaucer among others and inflected with a kind of silent laughter: the *Consolation of Philosophy*. In something akin to a dream vision, the figure of Philosophy appears to the all-too-human Boethius, imprisoned and awaiting execution on a political charge. Acting like a physician, she works to cure the captive of his illusions by removing his trust from worldly things and making him the master of himself. The situation itself calls forth the classic satiric attitudes of ridicule and scorn (transitory things are worthless) as well as questions so searching they can never really be answered to human satisfaction. Seeing that convinced Marxists are, or were, in the habit of interpreting incorrect thought as a psychiatric condition and liberty as collective self-mastery,[27] and that this liberty turns out to be very like a prison, considering too the founder's own outbreaks of scorn and ridicule, perhaps we can say that Marxism closes, dogmatizes, the uniquely open potential of a satire and a class of satires notable for bold questioning and, as Bakhtin puts it, freedom of invention.[28] The dialectical or back-and-forth structure of Boethian satire gives way to the Marxist dialectic which in its scientific power "seizes you on all sides as in a vise."[29] In Orwell's version of a doomed captive subjected to a mental examination, Philosophy has become the Stalinist O'Brien; Smith has been in his grip even when he imagined himself free.

With Boethius we enter a tradition that searches the deluded mind well before this practice was adopted by the doctors of "false consciousness." The pilgrim Chaucer, so beguiled by his companions, belongs to the tradition, as does Everyman, who must shed his illusions to meet death. Tolstoy's *Death of Ivan Ilych*, telling as it does of an examining magistrate compelled to examine himself as death approaches, has something of *Everyman* in it;[30] while that mighty Menippea *The Brothers Karamazov* contains elements of the *Consolation of Philosophy* itself. In the hands of ideologues who classify dissent as mental illness, the practice of searching error takes a different turn. In all likelihood the special attractions of satire to the ideologue lie in its way of radicalizing the attack on error, going to its very sources in the human brain.[31]

This study began by likening myth and satire, each a strong bonding force and a font of literary potential. Possibly it is because of this underlying similarity that Marxists were able to draw so powerfully on both modes at once, offering a vision of the classless society or earthly paradise even as they exposed the delusions of others with ridicule and wrath. But perhaps any creed with roots both in the Enlightenment, with its love of satire, and romanticism, with its revival of myth, has something of this dual character. For that matter, the *Consolation of Philosophy* itself alternates between poems of mythic tenor and the prose analysis of philosophical questions.

*

For examples of satire that invites and yet resists reduction to an ideological program we needn't look as far as Boethius. Imagine a reader of Dostoevsky, the reinventer of Menippean satire, who takes his work as a writ of chauvinist reaction. Imagine one who finds in Swift's fable of the horses a justification for slavery, eugenics, and the ridding of everything dirty and frivolous; who reduces Austen to snobbery, Dickens to do-gooding, Orwell to anti-intellectualism. In each case there is something to support these constructions, yet the reader has somehow missed the crux of the matter by ignoring qualities of the original in favor of a reductive simplification. The flight from freedom is a theme of Dostoevsky, Dickens, Orwell themselves. It is also a theme of modernity as such, for, ironically, it is out of satire that our formulas of argument are largely taken.

Notes

Introduction

1. Hannah Arendt, *The Human Condition* (Chicago: University of Chicago Press, 1958), pp. 200–1.

2. Gunther Barth, *City People: The Rise of Modern City Culture in Nineteenth-Century America* (New York: Oxford University Press, 1980), ch. 3.

3. Cited in Rochelle Gurstein, *The Repeal of Reticence* (New York: Hill and Wang, 1996), p. 158.

4. Alain Le Sage, *Le Diable boiteux,* translated as *Asmodeus; or The Devil Upon Two Sticks* (New York: Worthington, 1890), pp. 13–14.

5. M. M. Bakhtin, *The Dialogic Imagination*, tr. Caryl Emerson and Michael Holquist (Austin: University of Texas Press, 1981), p. 163. Ironically, the Cupid and Psyche story for which *The Golden Ass* is best known cautions against prying. In Roger Shattuck, *Forbidden Knowledge* (San Diego: Harcourt Brace and Company, 1996), it is read as a parable of transgressive knowledge.

6. Mikhail Bakhtin, *Problems of Dostoevksy's Poetics*, tr. Caryl Emerson (Minneapolis: University of Minnesota Press, 1984), p. 118.

7. On the routinization of the exposé see Kenneth Burke, *On Symbols and Society*, ed. Joseph R. Gusfield (Chicago: University of Chicago Press, 1989), p. 261: "A group of mere epigones have been cashing in on [Bentham's genius for debunking] for a century, bureaucratizing his imaginative inventions in various kinds of 'muckraking' enterprises." Dickens would argue with "imaginative."

8. Robert M. Adams, *The Roman Stamp: Frame and Facade in Some Forms of Neo-Classicism* (Berkeley: University of California Press, 1974), p. 22.

9. Ian Watt, *The Rise of the Novel* (Berkeley: University of California Press, 1957), p. 23.

10. Robert Darnton, *The Literary Underground of the Old Regime* (Cambridge, Mass.: Harvard University Press, 1982), ch. 1.

11. Bakhtin, *Dialogic Imagination*, p. 163.

12. Cited in Gurstein, *Repeal of Reticence*, p. 202.

13. James Joyce, *Ulysses* (Oxford: Oxford University Press, 1993), p. 577.

14. Northrop Frye, *Anatomy of Criticism* (New York: Atheneum, 1967), p. 229. "But if a writer should be quite consistent, / How could he possibly show things existent?" Byron, *Don Juan*, Canto XV, stanza 87. Cf. the "Digression in

the Modern Kind" in Swift's *Tale of a Tub*: "I cannot but bewail that no famous *modern* hath ever yet attempted an universal system, in a small portable volume, of all things that are to be known, or believed, or imagined, or practised in life." *A Tale of a Tub and Other Works* (Oxford: Oxford University Press, 1986), p. 60.

15. Leonard Feinberg, "Satire: The Inadequacy of Recent Definitions," *Genre* 1 (1968), 31–37.

16. Richard Holmes, "Voltaire's Grin," *New York Review of Books*, Nov. 30, 1995, p. 49. If, however, freedom of speech is understood as a quest for "truth," then with the attainment of truth, or the propagation of error, freedom of speech may stop. And so, according to Michael Oakeshott, "If we want instruction about the theory of liberal-democratic freedom of speech it is not to Milton or to Mill that we should go, but to Montaigne and Hume." Michael Oakeshott, *Religion, Politics and the Moral Life* (New Haven: Yale University Press, 1993), p. 117. Montaigne's great essay "On Experience" concludes satirically, "Upon the highest throne in the world, we are seated, still, upon our arses." Michel de Montaigne, *Essays*, tr. M. A. Screech (London: Penguin, 1993), p. 426.

17. Stewart Justman, *The Psychological Mystique* (Evanston: Northwestern University Press, 1998).

18. Kenneth Burke, *A Grammar of Motives* (Berkeley: University of California Press, 1969), p. 97.

19. Satiric ridicule of academies and the scholastic style (and a kind of general travesty of scholastic pro and contra is staged in the *Canterbury Tales*) reflects a feeling that their formulas capture nothing but air.

20. J. Glenn Gray, *The Warriors* (New York: Harper and Row, 1970), p. 133.

21. In asserting the common identity of all workers in *The Communist Manifesto*—a bill of indictment of the bourgeois order—Marx uses a highly satiric style.

22. In other precursors of the modern news—the sixteenth-century ballad (also termed "news") and seventeenth-century papers used as instruments of political warfare—the element of factuality is weak. See Lennard J. Davis, *Factual Fictions: The Origins of the English Novel* (Philadelphia: University of Pennsylvania Press, 1996), ch. 3 and 4.

23. Joyce to Arthur Power, in *Conversations with James Joyce*, ed. Clive Hart (Chicago: University of Chicago Press, 1982), p. 98. Hence too the dashing of illusions against the rocks of the real in *Dubliners*.

24. Alvin B. Kernan, *The Plot of Satire* (New Haven: Yale University Press, 1965), p. 200.

25. Jill Mann, *Chaucer and Medieval Estates Satire* (Cambridge, U.K.: Cambridge University Press, 1973), p. 9.

26. Adam Smith, *Lectures on Rhetoric and Belles Lettres* (Indianapolis: Liberty Classics, 1985), p. 8. On this view, Swift's own writing suffers something of the fate to which he condemns modern productions. "Such a jest there is that will not pass out of Covent Garden, and such a one that is nowhere intelligible but at Hyde Park corner." See the Preface to *A Tale of a Tub*, p. 20.

27. Helen Cooper, *Oxford Guides to Chaucer: The Canterbury Tales* (Oxford: Oxford University Press, 1991), p. 98. The high point of the Miller's Tale is a unique twist of circumstance, an unrepeatable moment, a singularity. Hardy's "Satires of Circumstance" isolate just such moments of intense irony, now stripped of comedy. Significantly, these poems bear "local" titles, titles of place: "In the Room of the Bride-Elect," "Outside the Window," "At the Draper's."

28. Feinberg, "Inadequacy," p. 36.

29. Kernan, *Plot of Satire*, p. 5.

30. Though "satire" doesn't derive from "satyr," Hamlet's "Hyperion to a satyr" helps mark him a satirist.

31. If satire at its most aggressive produces an effect like a drama of accusation, the Grand Inquisitor episode is just that.

32. Darnton, *Literary Underground*, ch. 1.

33. Swift, *A Tale of a Tub*, p. 84.

34. By the same token, a parody too good may get itself mistaken for an original. In a Swiftian hoax that became one of the events of Australian literary history, two poets out to demolish the pretensions of modernism passed off their own counterfeit as the poems of the unknown genius Ern Malley. The authorities who prosecuted the publisher for indecency took a more literal view of the crimes of modernism. That the poems took on a life and legend of their own, contrary to their creators' intentions, is a uniquely ironic illustration of satiric freedom. See Michael Heyward, *The Ern Malley Affair* (St. Lucia: University of Queensland Press, 1993).

35. Joyce, *Ulysses*, p. 402.

36. Joyce, *Ulysses*, p. 114.

37. Gary Saul Morson, "Prosaic Bakhtin: *Landmarks*, Anti-Intelligentsialism, and the Russian Counter-Tradition," *Common Knowledge* 2 (1993), 57. See Bakhtin's account of the Menippean tradition in *Problems of Dostoevsky's Poetics*.

38. Benjamin Franklin, *Writings* (New York: Library of America, 1987), p. 25.

39. On the civilizing process see Norbert Elias, *The History of Manners*, tr. Edmund Jephcott (New York: Pantheon, 1978); and *Power and Civility*, tr. Edmund Jephcott (New York: Pantheon, 1982). Both originally published 1939.

40. Jürgen Habermas, *The Structural Transformation of the Public Sphere: An Inquiry into a Category of Bourgeois Society*, tr. Thomas Burger and Frederick Lawrence (Cambridge, Mass.: MIT Press, 1991), pp. 60–61.

41. The title of National Public Radio's flagship show, *All Things Considered*, also has satiric connections. "I can't say that it puzzles me at all, / If all things be considered," says Byron in *Don Juan* (Canto II, stanza 3).

42. Byron, *Don Juan*, Canto XVI, stanza 3: "My tale is / De rebus cunctis et quibusdam aliis."

43. Consider also the multiplicity of Swift's targets. "A good Lucianic satire attempts to make as many simultaneous points as possible—the more different aspects of an evil the satiric symbol catches the better; and in this sense Swift's pre-eminence as a satirist is obvious." Ronald Paulson, *The Fictions of Satire* (Baltimore: Johns Hopkins University Press, 1967), p. 155. That *A Tale of a Tub* somehow overflows into two other works, "The Battle of the Books" and "The Mechanical Operation of the Spirit," is another example of Swiftian excess.

44. Harold Rosenberg, *Act and the Actor* (Chicago: University of Chicago Press, 1970), p. 76.

45. Daniel Defoe, *Moll Flanders* (New York: Crowell, 1970), p. 150.

46. James Joyce, "Daniel Defoe," ed. and tr. Joseph Prescott, *Buffalo Studies* 1 (1964), 3–25.

47. On two lines of the European novel, see Bakhtin, *Dialogic Imagination*, p. 366f. The prose of the second line seems to originate in "the process of a free (that is, reformulating) translation of others' works" (p. 378; entire passage italicized in the original). As is well known, this was Chaucer's method of composition.

48. Bakhtin, *Dialogic Imagination*, p. 49.

49. On the link between Chaucer's gothic and "modern fragmented art and literature," see D. S. Brewer, "The Fabliaux," in *Companion to Chaucer Studies*, ed. Beryl Rowland (New York: Oxford University Press, 1979), p. 310.

50. Asa Briggs, *Victorian People* (Chicago: University of Chicago Press, 1972), p. 93.

51. Richard Ellmann, *The Consciousness of Joyce* (Toronto: Oxford University Press, 1977), p. 78.

52. Anthony Trollope, *An Autobiography* (London: Oxford University Press, 1953), p. 35.

53. Jerome J. McGann, *DON JUAN in Context* (Chicago: University of Chicago Press, 1976), p. 70.

54. *Dickens' Journalism*, Vol. 2: *"The Amusements of the People" and Other Papers* (London: Dent, 1996), p. xvii.

55. Frye, *Anatomy of Criticism*, p. 311.

56. Bakhtin, *Dialogic Imagination*, p. 376.

57. Ellmann, *Joyce's Consciousness*, p. 83. "On now. Dare it": Joyce, *Ulysses*, p. 139. The anger in Stephen's character as angry young man harks back not only to Hamlet's sarcasms but perhaps, through Swift, to Juvenal, as the angry Ivan Karamazov invokes Juvenal with his cry in court of *"Panem et circenses."* Juvenal, Swift, Stephen Dedalus: three tonalities of the anger of exile.

58. Among the stranger modes of exaggeration of the present moment is the fashion for present-tense fiction: "I walk into the room, I pour a cup of coffee," as though a self-dramatizing ego were in revolt against the past tense of traditional narrative. In doing away with retrospect, this sort of shutter-click prose, with its snapshot of a moment that is always the present, also does away with depth perception.

59. James R. Kincaid, *The Novels of Anthony Trollope* (Oxford: Clarendon Press, 1977), p. 164.

60. Joyce, *Ulysses*, p. 713.

61. Simon Leys, *Chinese Shadows* (Harmondsworth, Middlesex: Penguin, 1978), p. 167.

62. Albert O. Hirschman, *The Rhetoric of Reaction: Perversity, Futility, Jeopardy* (Cambridge, Mass.: Harvard University Press, 1991).

63. Rakitin in *The Brothers Karamazov*, meddlesome, inquisitive, opportunistic, already making a name for himself as a journalist, belongs to the same group.

64. Henry James, *The Reverberator* (New York: Grove, n.d.), p. 14.

65. James, *The Reverberator*, p. 160.

66. There is a trace of the stoic-satiric tradition of the Enlightenment in Bloom's contemplation of his wife's infidelity with "the apathy of the stars" (p. 686). He returns immediately to Mother Earth.

67. An interesting figure in this connection is Bentham, in whom satire yields to political mechanics and psychological reductions.

68. Joyce, *Ulysses*, p. 686. Cf. the cosmic insignificance of the affair of the lock in "The Rape of the Lock."

69. Ian Watt, "The Ironic Tradition in Augustan Prose from Swift to Johnson," in Ian Watt and James R. Sutherland, *Restoration and Augustan Prose* (Los

Angeles: University of California, William Andrews Clark Memorial Library, 1956), p. 28.

Chapter 1

1. M. M. Bakhtin, *The Dialogic Imagination*, tr. Caryl Emerson and Michael Holquist (Austin: University of Texas Press, 1981), p. 323. Bakhtin's cardinal insight—that our words are directed to the words of others—would have brought no surprise to a poet whose every line seems a response to something already written. Bakhtin's discovery was Chaucer's practice.

2. Karl Mannheim, *Ideology and Utopia*, tr. Louis Wirth and Edward Shils (New York: Harcourt, Brace and World, 1936), pp. 8–9.

3. *The Parliament of Fowls* ends inconclusively; *The House of Fame* and *The Canterbury Tales* are incomplete.

4. On hero and role, surplus potential, and so on, see Bakhtin, *Dialogic Imagination*, p. 37. In theorizing about the novel and its free investigation of the world, Bakhtin is always close to satire.

5. Apuleius, *The Golden Ass*, tr. Robert Graves (New York: Noonday, 1967), p. 204.

6. This opposition itself can be made too schematic.

7. General Prologue, ll. 730–35, in Geoffrey Chaucer, *Works*, ed. F. N. Robinson (Boston: Houghton Mifflin, 1957). Subsequent references are given in my text.

8. Alice S. Miskimin, *The Renaissance Chaucer* (New Haven: Yale University Press, 1975), p. 83.

9. In his pretense of tidying up Moll Flanders's own words, Defoe—a master of the illusion of report—makes a kind of fictive concession to propriety. If Defoe's teasing cautions and disclaimers place him in the tradition of Chaucer, the marital career of Moll Flanders necessarily recalls the Wife of Bath.

10. Larry Benson, "Geoffrey Chaucer and Courtly Speech," unpublished paper, p. 16.

11. Kenneth Burke, *A Grammar of Motives* (Berkeley: University of California Press, 1969), pp. 87–98.

12. On idioms in Chaucer's fabliaux see Beryl Rowland, "What Chaucer Did to the Fabliau," *Studia Neophilologica* 51 (1979), 208–9.

13. Swift's "Battle of the Books" took place "last Friday" in St. James Library. Time and place are accounted for. For what it may be worth, the Miller's Tale is also a tale of a tub.

14. Bakhtin, *Dialogic Imagination*, p. 378. The assignment of a "proper" style to a number of speakers marks the relativization of language that points the true course of European prose in Bakhtin's account. As Bakhtin tells it, once language itself is set at a certain distance from the author—moving off center, as it were—the text acquires an inflection of smiling irony (p. 377). Hence Chaucer.

15. *The Decameron*, tr. Mark Musa and Peter E. Bondanella (New York: Norton, 1977), p. 145.

16. Some idea of the formulaic nature of the "realistic" defense can be derived from Rochelle Gurstein, *The Repeal of Reticence* (New York: Hill and Wang, 1996).

17. With Chaucer and Boccaccio we can speak of a humanist defense of artistic liberty. In Ben Jonson's *Bartholmew Fair*, with its sharp ridicule of Puritan objections to the theater itself, humanism goes on the offensive. I mention this work, first because by making a satiric issue of the Puritan campaign against the stage it confirms the debt freedom of expression owes to satire. Additionally, though, its plenteous cast (some three dozen speaking roles) and accentuation of the middle class, its exposure of fraud, its slanging matches and projected reconciliation of all at a final supper, loosely evoke the *Canterbury Tales*.

18. Charles Leslie, cited in John Dunn, *Western Political Theory in the Face of the Future* (Cambridge, U.K.: Cambridge University Press, 1993), p. 4.

19. Mikhail Bakhtin, *Rabelais and His World*, tr. Hélène Iswolsky (Bloomington: Indiana University Press, 1984), p. 81. Bakhtin underlines "the essential relation of festive laughter to time and to the change of seasons" (pp. 80–81). As everyone knows, the *Canterbury Tales* opens with a salute to the new season.

20. Bakhtin, *Dialogic Imagination*, p. 377.

21. Ronald Paulson, *The Fictions of Satire* (Baltimore: Johns Hopkins University Press, 1967), pp. 38, 136.

22. Mikhail Bakhtin, *Problems of Dostoevsky's Poetics*, tr. Caryl Emerson (Minneapolis: University of Minnesota Press, 1984), p. 91.

23. Lennard J. Davis, *Factual Fictions: The Origins of the English Novel* (Philadelphia: University of Pennsylvania Press, 1996). In Middleton's *A Trick to Catch the Old One*—a satire on the moral squalor of social climbing, land-grabbing, financiering, and capitalism generally—the air swarms with rumors that are called news but are without verity.

24. *Merchant of Venice*, III.i. 6–10.

25. Stewart Justman, "Trade as Pudendum: Chaucer's Wife of Bath," *Chaucer Review* 28 (1994), 344–52.

26. Derek Brewer, "Gothic Chaucer," in *Geoffrey Chaucer*, ed. Brewer (Athens: Ohio University Press, 1975), p. 11.

27. Addison's publication of letters to the editor possibly of his own composition is also in the tradition of Chaucerian reporting.

28. Bakhtin, *Problems of Dostoevsky's Poetics*, p. 30.

29. James Boswell, *The Life of Samuel Johnson* (New York: Knopf, 1992), p. 90.

30. Boswell, *Life of Johnson*, p. 90.

31. In his very journalism Dickens sometimes turned the floor over to fictive characters. In the case of the rather carnivalesque King of the Bill-Stickers, Dickens plays the role of the recorder taking down every word. "These are the minutes of my conversations with His Majesty, as I noted them down afterwards. I am not aware that I have been betrayed into any alteration or suppression." *Dickens' Journalism*, Vol. 2: *"The Amusements of the People" and Other Papers* (London: Dent, 1996), p. 349.

32. Harold Bloom, *The Western Canon* (New York: Harcourt Brace and Company, 1994), p. 193.

33. Letter to Grant Richards, 5 May 1906, in *Letters of James Joyce*, ed. Richard Ellmann, Vol. II (New York: Viking, 1966), p. 134.

Chapter 2

1. Marilyn Butler, *Romantics, Rebels and Reactionaries: English Literature and Its Background, 1760–1830* (Oxford: Oxford University Press, 1981), p. 70.

2. Seeing that any given style "edits" reality in the sense of playing things up or down in accordance with its own program, it seems fitting that modern civic journalism originates in the critical refinement of style. The power of literary styles to edit the world in their own image is parodically celebrated in the "Oxen of the Sun" episode of *Ulysses*, where in recommending his public-spirited scheme to increase the population, "Mr Mulligan . . . made court to the scholarly by an apt quotation from the classics which, as it dwelt upon his memory seemed to him a sound and tasteful support of his contention." Sound and tasteful: this is the ethos of Addison. James Joyce, *Ulysses* (Oxford: Oxford University Press, 1993), p. 384. See also Wolfgang Iser, *The Implied Reader: Patterns of Communication in Prose Fiction from Bunyan to Beckett* (Baltimore: Johns Hopkins University Press, 1974), ch. 7.

3. John Milton, *Complete Prose Works*, Vol. 2 (New Haven: Yale University Press, 1959), p. 565.

4. Spectator No. 34, in *The Spectator*, ed. Donald Bond, 5 vols. (Oxford: Oxford University Press, 1965). Subsequent references are given in my text. Capitalization is regularized.

5. Preface to "Fables Ancient and Modern," in John Dryden, *Works*, Vol. 11 (Edinburgh: William Patterson, 1882), pp. 208–44.

6. Jürgen Habermas, *The Structural Transformation of the Public Sphere: An Inquiry into a Category of Bourgeois Society*, tr. Thomas Burger and Frederick Lawrence (Cambridge, Mass.: MIT Press, 1991), p. 43.

7. Louis Wirth, as cited in Jill Mann, *Chaucer and Medieval Estates Satire* (Cambridge, U.K.: Cambridge University Press, 1973), p. 292.

8. M. M. Bakhtin, *The Dialogic Imagination*, tr. Caryl Emerson and Michael Holquist (Minneapolis: University of Minnesota Press, 1984), p. 14.

9. Larry Benson, "Geoffrey Chaucer and Courtly Speech," unpublished ms.

10. Bakhtin, *Dialogic Imagination*, p. 384.

11. Addison, as I've said, wants to fortify sociability with moral content. For Austen it is better to have morals without manners (Darcy) than the reverse. A lack of manners is reformable. Besides, the smooth manners of the man without morals prove to be no manners at all, a point also instanced by Ferdinand Lopez in Trollope's *The Prime Minister*.

12. Leonard W. Levy, *Emergence of a Free Press* (New York: Oxford University Press, 1985), p. 12.

13. Hence perhaps Adam Smith's use of Addison in his lectures on style. See Smith, *Lectures on Rhetoric and Belles Lettres* (Indianapolis: Liberty Classics, 1985).

14. Norbert Elias, *Power and Civility*, tr. Edmund Jephcott (New York: Pantheon, 1982; originally published 1939), p. 310. The civilizing process concerns not only the finer points of manners but also, first of all, the reduction of brutality and the concentration of the means of violence in the hands of a central power. Addison's opposition to dueling, as in Spectator No. 99, thus identifies him as a partisan of the civilizing process.

15. On the benignity of commerce, see Albert O. Hirschman, *The Passions and the Interests: Political Arguments for Capitalism before Its Triumph* (Princeton: Princeton University Press, 1977). For Addison's views of commerce, see Spectator No. 69.

16. See Addison's *Cato*, Act I, Scene IV.

17. Elias, *Power and Civility*, p. 297.

18. Gerald Bruns, *Inventions: Writing, Textuality, and Understanding in Literary History* (New Haven: Yale University Press, 1982), p. 11.

19. Bruns, *Inventions*, p. 11.

20. Friedrich Engels, *The Condition of the Working Class in England*, tr. W. O. Henderson and W. H. Chaloner (Stanford: Stanford University Press, 1958), p. 331.

21. Swift, Preface to the "Battle of the Books."

22. Swift, "Verses on the Death of Dr. Swift," ll. 460–62.

23. Dryden, "Discourse concerning the Original and Progress of Satire," in *Works*, Vol. 13, p. 98. Still standing after a stroke from the Green Knight, Gawain perhaps feels satirized.

24. Northrop Frye, *Anatomy of Criticism* (New York: Atheneum, 1967), p. 156.

25. See Alexandre Beljame, *Le Public el les hommes de lettres en Angleterre au dix-huitième siècle, 1660–1744;* cited by Bond, *Spectator,* Vol. I, p. lxxxviii.

26. When Addison's coauthor cites the same fable of the lion and the painter as the Wife of Bath, making the same point that stories would look different if women and not their slanderers wielded the pen (Spectator No. 11), the effect is different. It is as though Steele were expurgating the Wife.

27. In and of itself, the chain of descent from the Knight's Tale to the Reeve's makes a mockery of Theseus' chain of love.

28. In the easy motion of Addison's papers, moreover, we seem to read a parable of the "negative liberty"—the absence of external constraint—authorized by Locke. The "freedom to be oneself" enjoyed by members of the Spectator club and realized by Addison himself as a satirist released from formal conventions, is a tribute to Addison's philosophical mentor. "Freedom to be oneself": Ronald Paulson, *The Fictions of Satire* (Baltimore: Johns Hopkins University Press, 1967), p. 220.

29. Isaiah Berlin, *The Crooked Timber of Humanity* (New York: Vintage, 1992), p. 81.

30. See Stewart Justman, *The Psychological Mystique* (Evanston: Northwestern University Press, 1998).

31. Bakhtin, *Dialogic Imagination,* p. 163.

32. John Brewer, "Theater and Counter-Theater in Georgian Politics: The Mock Elections at Garrat," *Radical History Review* 22 (1979–80), 7–40.

33. Paul Strohm, *Social Chaucer* (Cambridge, Mass.: Harvard University Press, 1989), ch. 6.

34. Paulson, *Fictions of Satire,* p. 220.

35. Leo Braudy, *The Frenzy of Renown: Fame and Its History* (New York: Oxford University Press, 1986), p. 132. Byron remarkably, and uneasily, combined the satiric survey of the human scene with "individual action."

36. Hannah Arendt, *Lectures on Kant's Political Philosophy* (Chicago: University of Chicago Press, 1982), p. 55.

37. "The Function of Criticism at the Present Time," in *Poetry and Criticism of Matthew Arnold,* ed. A. Dwight Culler (Boston: Houghton Mifflin, 1961), p. 250.

The "easy and not too violently insisting" style "which the ancients so much admired" but which Arnold finds lacking in English newspapers of his day ("The Literary Influence of Academies," p. 273) defines Addison.

38. In the *Canterbury Tales* the Knight and the Parson—law and pulpit—are left unsatirized.

39. Joyce, *Ulysses*, p. 672.

40. In reflecting on "the pleasures derived from literature of instruction rather than of amusement as he himself had applied to the works of William Shakespeare more than once for the solution of difficult problems in imaginary or real life" (Joyce, *Ulysses*, p. 630), Bloom shows himself an Addisonian. Addison teaches his readers to derive pleasure from the literature of instruction. "Solaas" and "sentence" are the terms Chaucer would have used.

41. Cited in Bonamy Dobrée, *English Literature in the Early Eighteenth Century, 1700–1740* (Oxford: Clarendon Press, 1964), p. 456.

Chapter 3

1. John Locke, *Some Thoughts concerning Education* (Oxford: Clarendon Press, 1989), para. 66.

2. Jonathan Swift, *Prose Works*, Vol. 12 (Oxford: Basil Blackwell, 1955), p. 115. The last phrase seems to take indirect aim at refiners of taste like Addison. The narrator's profession of goodwill and public spirit mirrors that of Addison in his statement of satiric policy.

3. Steven Marcus, *Engels, Manchester, and the Working Class* (New York: Vintage, 1975), p. 17. The reasoner is Bentham.

4. In posing this question, the narrator seems to fuse with Swift momentarily, as the pilgrim Chaucer does with the poet at times.

5. Edmund Burke, *Reflections on the Revolution in France* (Indianapolis: Library of Liberal Arts, 1955), pp. 86–87.

6. Robert M. Adams, *The Roman Stamp: Frame and Facade in Some Forms of Neo-Classicism* (Berkeley: University of California Press, 1974), p. 153.

7. Swift's position seems almost as paradoxical as that of Joyce, who wrote always about a city he was estranged from.

8. Karl Mannheim, *Ideology and Utopia*, tr. Louis Wirth and Edward Shils (New York: Harcourt, Brace and World, 1936), p. 70. Swift's utopia, such as it is, is the land of the horses in *Gulliver's Travels*.

9. From the satiric to the doctrinaire isn't necessarily far. While both the *Fable of the Bees* and the "Essay on Charity and Charity-Schools" by Mandeville,

Swift's contemporary, are underwritten by the theory of mercantilism, the first is a work of Menippean license, the latter a kind of strict deduction from economic principles.

10. Where Swift takes us into the brain of the modern, a number of the *Canterbury Tales* reflect on their own teller—the weaver of the web.

11. Jonathan Swift, *A Tale of a Tub and Other Works* (Oxford: Oxford University Press, 1986), p. 16.

12. The Laputians in *Gulliver's Travels* are portrayed as addicted to news.

13. Defoe, *An Essay Upon Projects*, cited in Thomas L. Haskell, "Capitalism and the Origins of the Humanitarian Sensibility," *American Historical Review* 90 (1985), 558.

14. On Swift and Defoe, see Nigel Dennis, *Jonathan Swift: A Short Character* (New York: Macmillan, 1964), pp. 122–33.

15. Swift, *Tale of a Tub*, p. 84.

16. Swift, *Tale of a Tub*, p. 20.

17. Michael André Bernstein, *Bitter Carnival: Ressentiment and the Abject Hero* (Princeton: Princeton University Press, 1992), p. 105.

18. Hence Orwell takes care to establish sounds and smells at the beginning of *Nineteen Eighty-four.*

19. M. M. Bakhtin, *The Dialogic Imagination*, tr. Caryl Emerson and Michael Holquist (Austin: University of Texas Press, 1981), p. 223.

20. Dickens like Swift is a voice of generous indignation. This is the title of ch. 12 of Donald Bruce, *Radical Doctor Smollett* (Boston: Houghton Mifflin, 1965). The term "apparent objectivity" figures in this chapter.

21. Like the modern preface lengthier than the work that follows (a practice satirized in the Preface to *A Tale of a Tub*), the Wife of Bath's Prologue somewhat overshadows her own tale. Each case suggests an inversion of due order.

22. François Rabelais, *Gargantua and Pantagruel* (Harmondsworth, Middlesex: Penguin, 1955), p. 299.

23. Albert O. Hirschman, *The Passions and the Interests: Political Arguments for Capitalism before Its Triumph* (Princeton: Princeton University Press, 1977). Triggering the war between Picrochole and Grandgousier is the injury done to a party of shepherds who courteously ask some bakers to sell them bread at the market price.

24. Sympathy figures as a key term in Adam Smith's study of the Newtonian mechanics of civil society, the *Theory of Moral Sentiments*. Much as the roguery of Mandeville gives way to the civility of Smith, the dazzling self-command shown in Swift's straight-faced style is moralized into the stoicism of the *Moral Sentiments*.

25. Rabelais, *Gargantua and Pantagruel*, p. 74.

26. Bakhtin, *Dialogic Imagination*, p. 195.

27. Ronald Paulson, *The Fictions of Satire* (Baltimore: Johns Hopkins University Press, 1967), Part III. It is hard to think of the pilgrim Chaucer as anything but "middle" class, not that we know anything directly of his social position.

28. See Spectator No. 10, in *The Spectator*, ed. Donald Bond, 5 vols. (Oxford: Clarendon Press, 1965). On Swift on the few and the many, see Ian Watt, "The Ironic Tradition in Augustan Prose from Swift to Johnson," in Ian Watt and James R. Sutherland, *Restoration and Augustan Prose* (University of California, Los Angeles: William Andrews Clark Memorial Library, 1956).

29. Spectator No. 510.

30. See Stewart Justman, *The Psychological Mystique* (Evanston: Northwestern University Press, 1998). Where Addison brings philosophy out of closets and blends diverse individuals in a single club, Bernays puts ideas to work and promotes assimilation into the new consumer society.

31. The method of "indirect suggestion implicating self-interest" Bloom uses with Molly, Bernays uses with the nation. See James Joyce, *Ulysses* (Oxford: Oxford University Press, 1993), p. 639.

32. Chaucer's enrichment of the fabliau beyond any precedent; his endowing the Wife of Bath with a voice beyond that of her predecessor in the *Romance of the Rose*—voice enough to dispute with the clerical tradition; his substitution of a deeper tale for the one originally assigned the Wife (that is, the Shipman's)—all illustrate the quickening of satiric figures.

Chapter 4

1. Harold Bloom, *The Western Canon* (New York: Harcourt Brace and Company, 1994), p. 193.

2. Albert O. Hirschman, *The Rhetoric of Reaction: Perversity, Futility, Jeopardy* (Cambridge, Mass.: Harvard University Press, 1991), p. 44.

3. Gordon S. Wood, "Conspiracy and the Paranoid Style: Causality and Deceit in the Eighteenth Century," *William and Mary Quarterly*, Third Series, 39 (1982), 427.

4. Alvin B. Kernan, *The Plot of Satire* (New Haven: Yale University Press, 1965), p. 102.

5. Hirschman, *Rhetoric of Reaction*, pp. 11–12. Emphasis in the original.

6. Northrop Frye, *Anatomy of Criticism* (New York: Atheneum, 1967), p. 229.

7. David Miller, *Philosophy and Ideology in Hume's Political Thought* (Oxford: Clarendon Press, 1981), p. 200.

8. Liberals make heavy use of perversity arguments, claiming for example that the punitive approach to crime just makes things worse. It is "counterproductive."

9. Ronald Paulson, *Theme and Structure in Swift's Tale of a Tub* (Hamden, Conn.: Archon Press, 1972), ch. 2.

10. Isaiah Berlin, *Four Essays on Liberty* (London: Oxford University Press, 1969), p. 23.

11. John Brewer, "Theater and Counter-Theater in Georgian Politics: The Mock Elections at Garrat," *Radical History Review* 22 (1979–80), 19.

12. Lynn Hunt, *Politics, Culture, and Class in the French Revolution* (Berkeley: University of California Press, 1984), p. 109.

13. Robert Darnton, *The Literary Underground of the Old Regime* (Cambridge, Mass.: Harvard University Press, 1982), ch. 1.

14. Robin Evans, *The Fabrication of Virtue: English Prison Architecture, 1750–1840* (Cambridge, U.K.: Cambridge University Press, 1982), p. 198.

15. John Stuart Mill, *Autobiography* (Indianapolis: Library of Liberal Arts, 1957), pp. 43–44.

16. Friedrich Engels, *The Condition of the Working Class in England*, tr. and ed. W. O. Henderson and W. H. Chaloner (Stanford: Stanford University Press, 1958), p. 242.

17. Karl Marx, *The Communist Manifesto*, ed. Frederic L. Bender (New York: Norton, 1988), p. 72.

18. Consider too the Pardoner's performance. Seeking to slay death, the merrymakers in his tale are themselves slain, while the teller, vaunting his power, is struck impotent in the end.

19. Marx, *Communist Manifesto*, p. 69.

20. Richard Ellmann, *The Consciousness of Joyce* (Toronto: Oxford University Press, 1977), p. 78.

21. "Ever varying rhyme": Canto VII, stanza 2. On the political independence of the poet, see Canto IX, stanza 25: "I wish men to be free / As much from mobs as kings."

22. Ben Edwin Perry, *The Ancient Romances: A Literary-Historical Account of Their Origins* (Berkeley: University of California Press, 1967), p. 45.

23. Letter to Murray, August 12, 1819; cited in Jerome J. McGann, *DON JUAN in Context* (Chicago: University of Chicago Press, 1976), p. 1.

24. McGann, *DON JUAN in Context*, p. 99.

Chapter 5

1. William Wordsworth, Preface to the Second Edition of *Lyrical Ballads,* in *Selected Poems and Prefaces,* ed. Jack Stillinger (Boston: Houghton Mifflin, 1965), p. 449. Cf. Adam Smith's analysis of the causes of the laborer's mental "torpor" and loss of the habit of "exertion" in *The Wealth of Nations* (New York: Modern Library, 1937), p. 734. Smith's *Theory of Moral Sentiments* is predicated on the value of sympathy.

2. Wordsworth, Preface, p. 449.

3. Reverent in its very criticism of Wordsworth, Arnold's "The Function of Criticism at the Present Time" is like a sermon on the text "The world is too much with us."

4. On Jane Austen and the civilizing process: consider the descriptions of tableware and table manners in Fanny Price's home in *Mansfield Park.*

5. Ronald Paulson, *Satire and the Novel in Eighteenth-Century England* (New Haven: Yale University Press, 1967), p. 59.

6. Marilyn Butler, *Romantics, Rebels and Reactionaries: English Literature and Its Background 1760–1830* (Oxford: Oxford University Press, 1981).

7. Spectator No. 10, in *The Spectator,* ed. Donald Bond, 5 vols. (Oxford: Clarendon Press, 1965).

8. Marilyn Butler, *Jane Austen and the War of Ideas* (Oxford: Clarendon Press, 1975), ch. 9.

9. Spectator No. 57.

10. Jane Austen, *Emma,* in *Complete Novels of Jane Austen* (New York: Modern Library, n.d.), p. 1015.

11. Austen, *Mansfield Park,* in *Complete Novels,* p. 702.

12. On public questions Jane Austen maintains a close silence; but silence can be a kind of ironic eloquence. With its accusation of Christ, the Grand Inquisitor episode of *The Brothers Karamazov* transposes to a higher plane the case against God that Ivan Karamazov pieces together from atrocity stories in the newspapers. Like those stories, the Inquisitor seems to demand a reply, but he gets none. The accused says nothing, perhaps in the belief that any answer he might make would compromise his freedom. His silence at any rate conveys something of the same enigmatic force as, say, the parables of the gospels. Jane Austen makes her refusal to the newspapers directly, a refusal eloquent in the sense of saying more by saying less. She dismisses their demands with a smile not of love but of satiric contempt.

13. The other side of novelty is repetition.

14. Mary Wollstonecraft, *A Vindication of the Rights of Woman* (New York: Norton, 1988), p. 93. See my discussion in *The Autonomous Male of Adam Smith* (Norman: University of Oklahoma Press, 1993).

15. "In all the important preparations of the mind she was complete: being prepared for matrimony by an hatred of home, restraint, and tranquillity; by the misery of disappointed affection, and contempt of the man she was to marry." Austen, *Mansfield Park*, p. 591.

16. See, in addition to Marilyn Butler's *Jane Austen and the War of Ideas*, Claudia Johnson, *Jane Austen: Women, Politics and the Novel* (Chicago: University of Chicago Press, 1988).

17. Austen, *Emma*, p. 1000. Mrs. Churchill's husband, also never introduced, goes on the list of nullified males.

18. Leonard W. Levy, *Emergence of a Free Press* (New York: Oxford University Press, 1985), p. 12.

19. Austen, *Pride and Prejudice*, in *Complete Novels*, p. 452.

20. Austen, *Pride and Prejudice*, p. 452.

21. Elizabeth Bennet flares up with "astonishment and disdain" (p. 443) on being confronted by Lady Catherine with the report that she and Darcy are on the brink of marriage.

22. Ian Watt, "The Ironic Tradition in Augustan Prose from Swift to Johnson," in Ian Watt and James R. Sutherland, *Restoration and Augustan Prose* (University of California, Los Angeles: William Andrews Clark Memorial Library, 1956), p. 43f.

23. Norbert Elias, *Power and Civility*, tr. Edmund Jephcott (New York: Pantheon, 1982; originally published 1939), p. 297.

24. Jane Austen, *Northanger Abbey*, in *Complete Novels*, p. 1078. Some critics, ignoring the unrelenting irony of the narrative as a whole and *A Tale of a Tub*–like ironies of the discourse in which this passage appears, read it as a cut at Addison.

25. Austen, *Northanger Abbey*, p. 1124.

26. Samuel Johnson, *Lives of the English Poets*, Vol. I (London: Oxford University Press, 1933), p. 466.

27. See Richard Whately's review, originally published in 1821, reprinted in *Pride and Prejudice*, ed. Donald J. Gray (New York: Norton, 1966), pp. 316–21. The reviewer also commends Austen for removing herself from the narrative and more or less giving it over to dialogue among characters who speak *in* character. We recall the narrator of the *Canterbury Tales* turning the tales over to their tellers.

28. Lionel Trilling, *Sincerity and Authenticity* (Cambridge, Mass.: Harvard University Press, 1972), p. 82.

29. Butler, *Romantics, Rebels and Reactionaries,* p. 179.

30. Austen, *Emma,* p. 967.

31. Austen, *Emma,* p. 1012.

32. Some threads running from the Knight's Tale and *A Midsummer Night's Dream:* the figure of Theseus, the rites of May (IV.i.132–33 in Shakespeare), lovers all but indistinguishable, supernatural machinery, the staging of a theatrical event. The holiday atmosphere of *A Midsummer Night's Dream,* its sense of the season and concluding apology, pick up other aspects of the *Canterbury Tales.*

Chapter 6

1. Northrop Frye, *Anatomy of Criticism* (New York: Atheneum, 1967), p. 234. Like Byron in *Don Juan,* Dickens mixes pathos and ridicule and exposes the cant of the age, but in plotted tales, where Byron worked virtually without a design.

2. This most notably in *Don Quixote. Sir Gawain and the Green Knight* (in which a sorceress plots against Arthur's court) is a romance with a current of satire. In *Heart of Darkness,* too, a hero is taken from center to wilderness, there to be subjected to trials that shake his sense of self, the entire adventure enveloped in an atmosphere of dream—but here romance is overpowered by a tone of satiric derision and disgust.

3. Irving Howe, *A Critic's Notebook* (San Diego: Harcourt Brace and Company, 1994), p. 74.

4. On plot in Trollope, see James R. Kincaid, *The Novels of Anthony Trollope* (Oxford: Clarendon Press, 1977), ch. 2.

5. Mikhail Bakhtin, *Problems of Dostoevsky's Poetics,* ed. and tr. Caryl Emerson (Minneapolis: University of Minnesota Press, 1984), p. 277. Dr. Johnson remarks on Shakespeare's comparative indifference to plot. In *Ulysses* coincidence, that mechanism of the Dickens plot, is but a special case of a kind of universal "punning" in which unlikes converge; on which see Richard Ellmann, *The Consciousness of Joyce* (Toronto: Oxford University Press, 1977), p. 90f.

6. Chaucer also dialogizes his source material in the plain sense, turning the Shipman's and Nun's Priest's Tales, for example, into tales of verbal back-and-forth.

7. Charles Dickens, *Little Dorrit* (Harmondsworth, Middlesex: Penguin, 1967), pp. 53, 67. Subsequent page references are given in my text.

8. Bakhtin's early reflections on the hero's dependence on the author to "consummate" his story seem to run counter to his thinking on Dostoevsky.

9. Alexis de Tocqueville, *Democracy in America*, tr. Henry Reeve et al., Vol II (New York: Vintage, 1945), pp. 338–39.

10. Thomas Carlyle, *Past and Present* (Boston: Houghton Mifflin, 1965), pp. 18–19.

11. Beryl Rowland, "What Chaucer Did to the Fabliau," *Studia Neophilologica* 51 (1979), 205–13.

12. See Bakhtin's discussion of *Little Dorrit* in *The Dialogic Imagination*, tr. Caryl Emerson and Michael Holquist (Austin: University of Texas Press, 1981), p. 302f.

13. Flora "held forth in a most distracting manner on a chaos of subjects, in which mackerel, and Mr F.'s Aunt in a swing, had become entangled with cockchafers and the wine trade" (p. 747).

14. Howe, *A Critic's Notebook*, p. 145.

15. John Forster, *The Life of Charles Dickens*, Vol. 3 (London: Chapman and Hall, 1874), p. 137.

16. Lionel Trilling thought *Little Dorrit* the creation of an imagination "akin to that which created *Piers Plowman*." Trilling, "Little Dorrit," *Kenyon Review* 15 (1953), 589.

17. Tocqueville, *Democracy in America*, Vol. II, p. 141.

18. Jeremy Bentham, *Handbook of Political Fallacies* (New York: Apollo, 1971), p. 155.

19. Bentham, *Handbook of Political Fallacies*, p. 259.

20. Dickens, letter to W. C. Macready, cited in Introduction to *Little Dorrit*, p. 19.

21. Within *Little Dorrit* itself the act of inspection so important to Bentham that he made a principle of it takes the form of a rite of inanity. In the Marshalsea "the smugglers habitually consorted with the debtors"—the kind of promiscuity the Panopticon was intended to abolish—"except at certain constitutional moments when somebody came from some Office, to go through some form of overlooking something which neither he nor anybody else knew anything about" (p. 97).

22. *Dickens' Journalism*, Vol. 2: *'The Amusements of the People' and Other Papers* (London: Dent, 1996), p. xv.

23. "To coin money" may be a trace of the Drapier letters, "Merdle" a trace of Swiftian scatology. Bakhtin in his reading of this passage in *The Dialogic Imagination*, pp. 303–7, seems to miss the biblical reference.

24. Bakhtin, *Dialogic Imagination*, p. 306. It is Bakhtin's sense of the novel as a genre that everything in it is disputable.

25. John Stuart Mill, *On Liberty* (New York: Norton, 1975), p. 40. Cf. Swift's "Argument against Abolishing Christianity" as well as Tolstoy's description of

the Mass as a kind of dumb show in *Resurrection:* "And none of those present, from the inspector down to Maslova, seemed conscious of the fact that Jesus, whose name the priest repeated such a great number of times, whom he praised with all these curious expressions, had forbidden the very things that were being done there: that he had not only prohibited this meaningless much-speaking and the blasphemous incantation over the bread and wine, but had also, in the clearest words, forbidden men to call other men their master or pray in temples. . . ." *Resurrection,* tr. Louise Maude (Oxford: Oxford University Press, 1994), p. 149. In the passages of estranged description preceding this comment factual account and satire come to the same thing.

26. James Joyce, *Ulysses* (Oxford: Oxford University Press, 1993), p. 583.

27. The surplus of persons in Dickens is like the overstuffed catalogs of Rabelais. No doubt more direct correspondences exist, as between the horsemanship of Gymnaste and Sleary's people in *Hard Times.*

28. F. Anne Payne, *Chaucer and Menippean Satire* (Madison: University of Wisconsin Press, 1981), p. 35.

29. Hannah Arendt, *Crises of the Republic* (New York: Harcourt Brace Jovanovich, 1972), p. 39.

30. Arendt, *Crises of the Republic,* p. 7. In *Don Juan* things settle into a pattern until something unexpected happens and the pattern is destroyed.

31. On mercantilist dogma see Louis A. Landa, *Essays in Eighteenth-Century Literature* (Princeton: Princeton University Press, 1980). To the economists Swift says with the Wife of Bath, "The experience woot wel it is noght so."

32. Frye, *Anatomy of Criticism,* p. 230.

33. Frye, *Anatomy of Criticism,* p. 229. When the satiric preference for practice over doctrine is itself made a doctrine, it becomes conservatism. Perhaps one way to figure the relation between Rabelais and Dostoevsky, the two focal points of Bakhtin's thinking, is that the satiric energy of the first yields in part to the archconservatism of the second.

34. "Solution": *Marx's Concept of Man,* ed. Erich Fromm (New York: Frederick Ungar, 1968), p. 127. "Resolved mystery": cited in John Dunn, *Western Political Theory in the Face of the Future* (Cambridge, U.K.: Cambridge University Press, 1993), p. 11.

35. Dunn, *Western Political Theory,* p. 12.

Chapter 7

1. Cf. Edmund Bertram's attempt to hush publicity surrounding the play staged at Mansfield Park.

2. Anthony Trollope, *The Prime Minister* (Oxford: Oxford University Press, 1983), Vol. I, pp. 2–3.

3. With its blend of mordancy and romance—delicate in itself—Henry James's *The Reverberator* is similar in manner to Trollope. Here the journalist Flack behaves with the impudence of the parvenu. Also featuring the journalist as vulgarian is *The Bostonians*.

4. Introduction by John McCormick to *The Prime Minister*, p. xxi.

5. Cited in Bradford A. Booth, "Trollope and 'Little Dorrit,'" *The Trollopian* 2 (1948), 238.

6. But not only Trollope. A review in *Harper's Magazine* finds *The Way We Live Now* both a caricature and an all-too-accurate reflection of Victorian society. See *Harper's Magazine* 51 (October 1875), 754.

7. According to Ruskin, "The essential value and truth of Dickens's writings have been unwisely lost sight of by many thoughtful persons, merely because he presents his truth with some colour of caricature." *Unto This Last* (New York: Appleton-Century-Crofts, 1967), p. 16. As though he had brought on himself yet another unwelcome association with Dickens, Trollope seems to have felt that satiric excess endangered the essential truth of *The Way We Live Now*.

8. Reviews of *The Way We Live Now* are collected in Donald Smalley, *Trollope: The Critical Heritage* (London: Routledge & Kegan Paul, 1969).

9. Trollope, *The Prime Minister*, Vol. II, p. 92.

10. Trollope, *The Prime Minister*, Vol. II, p. 89.

11. Spectator No. 10, in *The Spectator*, ed. Donald Bond, 5 vols. (Oxford: Clarendon Press, 1965).

12. Anthony Trollope, *The Way We Live Now* (New York: Modern Library, 1984), p. 9.

13. Ronald Paulson, *The Fictions of Satire* (Baltimore: Johns Hopkins University Press, 1967), p. 23.

14. Trollope, *The Way We Live Now*, pp. 9–10.

15. See Frank Kermode's Introduction to the Penguin edition of *The Way We Live Now* (1994).

16. Anthony Trollope, *An Autobiography* (London: Oxford University Press, 1953), p. 305.

17. The Preface appears in Charles Dickens, *Little Dorrit* (Harmondsworth, Middlesex: Penguin, 1967), pp. 35–36.

18. Cited in Michael Löwy, *Redemption and Utopia: Jewish Libertarian Thought in Central Europe* (Stanford: Stanford University Press, 1992), p. 84.

19. James R. Kincaid, *The Novels of Anthony Trollope* (Oxford: Clarendon Press, 1977), p. 40.

20. On this point see George Levine, *The Realistic Imagination: English Fiction from Frankenstein to Lady Chatterley* (Chicago: University of Chicago Press, 1981), p. 187. On the practice of reviving characters from preceding works, see Henry James's Preface to *The Princess Casamassima*.

21. An unsigned review in the *Spectator* of June 26, 1875, faults *The Way We Live Now* for being "choked with characters." See Smalley, *Trollope: The Critical Heritage*, p. 397.

22. Trollope, *The Way We Live Now*, p. 492.

23. Ronald Paulson, *Satire and the Novel in the Eighteenth Century* (New Haven: Yale University Press, 1967), p. 301.

24. The partially ironic view taken of landed gentlemen who are the moral center of gravity in their works marks the difficulty of labeling Trollope and Austen politically. Trollope called himself a conservative liberal; Austen might perhaps be called an Addisonian Tory.

25. The satirist who complains too much makes it seem that "his satire springs rather from his own caustic nature than from the sins of the world in which he lives." Trollope, *Autobiography*, p. 160.

26. Betrayed, first because at the crisis of the tale the husband threatens his wife's life, second because by the end of the tale the wife has disappeared from the stage.

27. Trollope, *Autobiography*, p. 253.

28. Arthur O. Lovejoy, *Great Chain of Being* (Cambridge, Mass.: Harvard University Press, 1936), p. 247.

29. Lovejoy, *Great Chain of Being*, p. 247.

30. Trollope. *Autobiography*, p. 251.

31. Levine, *Realistic Imagination*, ch. 9.

32. See Paulson, *Fictions of Satire*, p. 120f.

33. Adam Smith, *The Theory of Moral Sentiments* (Indianapolis: Liberty Classics, 1982), p. 308f.

34. Orwell had misgivings over the most lurid section of *Nineteen Eighty-four*—Room 101.

Chapter 8

"The art of surfeit" is from James Joyce, *Ulysses* (Oxford: Oxford University Press, 1993), p. 193. Subsequent page references are given in my text.

1. Anthony Trollope, *An Autobiography* (London: Oxford University Press, 1953), p. 204. *Gulliver's Travels* combines episodic construction and an excess of the satiric intensity that troubled Trollope in *The Way We Live Now*.

2. On the matter of voice: Chaucer in reciting the *Canterbury Tales* presumably adopted such voices as the Pardoner (a kind of self-impersonator) and the Wife of Bath, who for a large part of her Prologue takes the voice of her husbands. Joyce's choice for a 1923 gramophone recording was a piece of oratorical magnificence, framed inside the words of another speaker, from the Aeolus episode of *Ulysses*. See Stuart Gilbert, *James Joyce's Ulysses: A Study* (New York: Knopf, 1934), p. 165n. The framing of a speech by John F. Taylor inside the words of Prof. MacHugh, themselves part of a larger conversation, is a Chaucerian proceeding in itself. Consider the multiple frames of the also oratorical Nun's Priest's Tale, in a way a précis of the *Canterbury Tales*.

3. Leo Braudy, *The Frenzy of Renown: Fame and Its History* (New York: Oxford University Press, 1986), p. 244.

4. Mikhail Bakhtin, *Problems of Dostoevsky's Poetics*, tr. Caryl Emerson (Minneapolis: University of Minnesota Press, 1984), p. 30.

5. James Joyce, *Dubliners* (New York: Penguin, 1992), pp. 109–11.

6. "A Modest Proposal" comes back more thematically in "Lestrygonians," with its motif of cannibalism. Where Swift called on the Irish to consume goods only of their own manufacture, Joyce supported a boycott of English goods.

7. Regarding the motif of the inquest, cf. the inquiry into the wreck of the *Patna* in *Lord Jim*. Jim "could have reproduced like an echo the moaning of the engineer for the better information of these men who wanted facts" (ch. 4).

8. Robert M. Adams, *Surface and Symbol: The Consistency of James Joyce's Ulysses* (New York: Oxford University Press, 1962), pp. xvi–xvii; on collage, p. 247. As Adams points out, about the only detail Joyce preserved in adapting "A Painful Case" from an account in the *Freeman's Journal* was the train (pp. 52–54).

9. Introduction to Anthony Trollope, *The Prime Minister* (Oxford: Oxford University Press, 1983), p. xx.

10. Trollope, *The Prime Minister*, Vol. I, pp. 36, 31.

11. One thinks too of *Madame Bovary*, a work that in effect ridicules those who sought to suppress it for its portrayal of female license.

12. M. H. Abrams, *Natural Supernaturalism: Tradition and Revolution in Romantic Literature* (New York: Norton, 1973), pp. 421–22.

13. Wife of Bath's Prologue, l. 771, in Geoffrey Chaucer, *Works*, ed. F. N. Robinson (Boston: Houghton Mifflin, 1957).

14. "Quoniam," the slang term for the female genitalia (Wife's Prologue, l. 608), is Latin for "because." According to Joyce himself, one of Molly Bloom's

keywords, "because," corresponds to the breasts. See *Selected Letters of James Joyce*, ed. Richard Ellmann (New York: Viking, 1975), p. 285.

15. On the diatribe and its proximity to the soliloquy, see Bakhtin, *Problems of Dostoevsky's Poetics*, p. 120.

16. Joyce, *Selected Letters*, p. 285.

17. M. M. Bakhtin, *Art and Answerability*, tr. Vadim Liapunov (Austin: University of Texas Press, 1990), p. 184.

18. Penelope herself reverses the caricature of female guile, using cunning to preserve, not betray, her husband's honor.

19. Northrop Frye, *Anatomy of Criticism* (New York: Atheneum, 1967), p. 229.

20. Frye, *Anatomy of Criticism*, p. 229.

21. According to Stephen Dedalus, Shakespeare himself was a cuckold. Stephen is necessarily unaware of the twisted threads of analogy running between Odysseus' meditated revenge, Hamlet's overmeditated revenge, and Bloom's indirect and evasive victory over his wife's suitor. The excess of consciousness in which Hamlet's will to revenge seems to get lost becomes in Bloom a profusion of inner speech.

22. Something of the same effect is felt in the beautiful story "Araby," where a satiric excess of languages—the magic word of the title itself, the cries and curses of the streets, the transposed discourse of devotion, a household maxim, snips of English voices, and more—works to satirize the protagonist himself. The narrator is ridiculous, but he is not just ridiculous.

23. Alexander Pope, *The Art of Sinking in Poetry*, in *Works*, Vol. X (London: John Murray, 1886), p. 366.

24. Ian Jack, *Augustan Satire: Intention and Idiom in English Poetry 1660–1750* (Oxford: Clarendon Press, 1952), p. 23.

25. Bakhtin, *Problems of Dostoevsky's Poetics*, p. 126.

26. In the other line of the Chaucer tradition, *The Way We Live Now* opens with Lady Carbury complaining in all insincerity about "the system of puffing."

27. An Aeolian tradition traces back from Joyce's god of wind to the magnification of the name of Merdle by the press in *Little Dorrit* to the Aeolists of *A Tale of a Tub* and Rabelais's Isle of the Winds. See also the self-puffery and swollen rhetoric—the belching of the heart (Summoner's Tale, l. 1934)—of Chaucer's hypocrites of religion.

28. What are we to make of the catalog of the most academic figures of rhetoric in the Aeolus episode? In a series of consecutive papers in the *Spectator* of May 1711, Addison looks into the nature of false wit, from the acrostic and the anagram (Bloom has dabbled in both) to paronomasia. That the entire

discussion is grounded on Locke's distinction between wit and judgment is one more mark of the writer's regard for Locke. "Aeolus" seems more in the spirit of Rabelais, with his crazy encyclopedism and parodies of the scholastic.

29. Manciple's Tale, l. 134.

30. Gustave Flaubert, *Madame Bovary*, tr. Mildred Marmur (New York: New American Library, 1964), p. 182.

31. If the Miller's Tale subverts the pretentious romance of the Knight, Byron began *Don Juan* with an anecdotal fabliau as a joke on the "vasty" romanticism of Wordsworth and Southey. See Jerome J. McGann, *DON JUAN in Context* (Chicago: University of Chicago Press, 1976), p. 59. This study begins with a parallel between *Don Juan* and the *Canterbury Tales*.

32. God, says Stephen, is "a shout in the street" (p. 34).

33. D. S. Brewer, "The Fabliaux," in *Companion to Chaucer Studies*, ed. Beryl Rowland (New York: Oxford University Press, 1979), p. 297.

34. See the inventory of Joyce's books in Richard Ellmann, *The Consciousness of Joyce* (Toronto: Oxford University Press, 1977).

35. Frye, *Anatomy of Criticism*, p. 229.

36. Wife of Bath's Prologue, l. 102.

37. Elaine Pagels, *Adam, Eve, and the Serpent* (New York: Vintage, 1989), p. 30.

38. Richard Poirier, "The Difficulties of Modernism and the Modernism of Difficulty," *Humanities in Society* 1 (1978), 277.

39. Frye, *Anatomy of Criticism*, p. 314.

Chapter 9

1. George Orwell, *Down and Out in Paris and London* (New York: Harcourt Brace Jovanovich, 1961), p. 70.

2. Friedrich Engels, *The Condition of the Working Class in England*, tr. W. O. Henderson and W. H. Chaloner (Stanford: Stanford University Press, 1958), p. 313.

3. The Miller's defiance of the Host and jabs at the romantic pretension of the Knight, the noblest of the company, invite us to interpret his tale as an act of insurrection. Some read it as a symbolic enactment of the Peasant Revolt of 1381. Yet the sexual morality of the Miller's Tale is traditional, even conservative, in the sense that the husband is deemed ridiculous for marrying outside his age group and for being totally unequal to his role in a patriarchal order.

4. The author himself classed *Nineteen Eighty-four* as a satire. See *Nineteen Eighty-four: Text, Sources, Criticism*, ed. Irving Howe (New York: Harcourt Brace Jovanovich, 1982), p. 287.

5. Cf. Stuart Hampshire, "The Tory Anarchist," *New York Review of Books*, Jan. 30, 1992, 10–12. A similar tag has been applied to none other than Jane Austen. Austen, writes Marilyn Butler, is a Tory radical whose Toryism predominates over her radicalism. See Butler, *Jane Austen and the War of Ideas* (Oxford: Clarendon Press, 1975), p. 165.

6. "Credit the inconceivable": lecture by Irving Howe at West Chester University, Oct. 7, 1983. In his remarks on Gandhi, Orwell parts ways with the saint who loves his own wife and children no more than humanity in general; at the end of *Gulliver's Travels* Swift seems to part ways with a Gulliver who hates his wife and children with the same hatred that comprehends all of humankind.

7. George Orwell, *Collected Essays, Journalism and Letters*, Vol. II (New York: Harcourt Brace Jovanovich, 1968), p. 24.

8. Louis A. Landa, *Essays in Eighteenth-Century Literature* (Princeton: Princeton University Press, 1980), p. 14.

9. Fittingly, "The Book" at the center of *Nineteen Eighty-four* is a kind of cracked image of the supertheory of James Burnham. For Orwell's estimate of Burnham see *Collected Essays, Journalism and Letters*, Vol. IV, p. 160f.

10. Lecture at West Chester University, Oct. 7, 1983.

11. Mikhail Bakhtin, *Problems of Dostoevsky's Poetics*, tr. Caryl Emerson (Minneapolis: University of Minnesota Press, 1984), pp. 118–19.

12. Bakhtin, *Problems of Dostoevsky's Poetics*, p. 118.

13. Orwell, *Nineteen Eighty-four*, p. 147.

14. F. Anne Payne, *Chaucer and Menippean Satire* (Madison: University of Wisconsin Press, 1981), p. 32.

15. Ronald Paulson, *The Fictions of Satire* (Baltimore: Johns Hopkins University Press, 1967), p. 38.

16. Orwell, *Nineteen Eighty-four*, p. 169.

17. Northrop Frye, *Anatomy of Criticism* (New York: Atheneum, 1967), p. 229.

18. George Orwell, *Homage to Catalonia* (New York: Harcourt Brace Jovanovich, 1952), p. 104.

19. *Selected Satires of Lucian*, tr. Lionel Casson (New York: Norton, 1968), pp. 198, 201.

20. Mikhail Bakhtin, *Rabelais and His World*, tr. Hélène Iswolsky (Bloomington: Indiana University Press, 1984), p. 70.

21. Orwell, *Homage to Catalonia*, p. 18.

22. On the power of satiric laughter itself to "heal" and renew, see Bakhtin, *Rabelais and His World*, p. 70.

23. On "genre memory," see Gary Saul Morson and Caryl Emerson, *Mikhail Bakhtin: Creation of a Prosaics* (Stanford: Stanford University Press, 1990), pp. 295–97.

24. Bakhtin, *Problems of Dostoevsky's Poetics*, p. 138. Cf. Orwell's carnivalesque description of a Paris bistro in *Down and Out*, pp. 9–10.

25. On the logic of a single idea as the power driving totalitarian thought, see the conclusion of Hannah Arendt, *Totalitarianism* (Part Three of *The Origins of Totalitarianism*) (New York: Harcourt Brace and World, 1968).

26. Herzen as cited in Isaiah Berlin, *The Crooked Timber of Humanity* (New York: Vintage, 1992), p. 16.

27. Alvin B. Kernan, *The Plot of Satire* (New Haven: Yale University Press, 1965), p. 102.

28. Berlin, *Crooked Timber*, p. 237.

29. Orwell, *Collected Essays, Journalism and Letters*, Vol. IV, p. 139.

30. In fact, ideology at its most dogmatic—totalitarian ideology—acts like a satirist both blinded and possessed by his vision of a concealed truth.

31. Gary Saul Morson, "Prosaic Bakhtin: *Landmarks*, Anti-Intelligentsialism, and the Russian Counter-Tradition," *Common Knowledge* 2 (1993), 60.

32. Lionel Trilling, Introduction to *Homage to Catalonia*, p. v.

33. Mikhail Bakhtin, *The Dialogic Imagination*, tr. Caryl Emerson and Michael Holquist (Austin: University of Texas Press, 1981), p. 25.

Afterword

1. Jill Mann, "Chaucer and the Medieval Latin Poets: The Satiric Tradition," in *Geoffrey Chaucer*, ed. Derek Brewer (Athens: Ohio University Press, 1975), pp. 182–83.

2. George Steiner, *On Difficulty and Other Essays* (New York: Oxford University Press, 1978), p. 136.

3. Gerald Bruns, *Inventions: Writing, Textuality, and Understanding in Literary History* (New Haven: Yale University Press, 1982), p. 9.

4. Samuel Johnson, Preface to *Dictionary of the English Language* (London, 1755; rpt. AMS Press, 1967), p. 9.

5. Bruns, *Inventions*, p. 8.

6. The figure of the remarrying widow, whose literary archetype is the widow of Ephesus, appears in comic form in the Wife of Bath, in tragic form in Gertrude.

7. M. M. Bakhtin, *The Dialogic Imagination*, tr. Caryl Emerson and Michael Holquist (Austin: University of Texas Press, 1981), p. 55.

8. Perhaps Chaucer's understanding that human experience cannot fit in a single "high and straightforward" genre accounts for what Matthew Arnold deemed his deficiency of high seriousness. Even the principle that individuals in the novel cannot be identical with their role (lest they simply coincide with themselves) has its counterpart in Chaucer. Think of the disparity between the Prioress and her role. The Wife of Bath is called a Wife when she isn't even married. On the nonidentity of individual and role, see Bakhtin, *Dialogic Imagination*, p. 37.

9. The ablest American interpreter of Bakhtin: Gary Saul Morson. "Living an ordinary life": F. Anne Payne, *Chaucer and Menippean Satire* (Madison: University of Wisconsin Press, 1981), p. 202.

10. Gary Saul Morson, *Narrative and Freedom: The Shadows of Time* (New Haven: Yale University Press, 1994).

11. Jerome J. McGann, *DON JUAN in Context* (Chicago: University of Chicago Press, 1976), e.g., pp. 99–102.

12. Adam Smith, *The Wealth of Nations* (New York: Modern Library, 1937), p. 650. Smith would surely agree with Byron that "Few mortals know what end they would be at" (*Don Juan*, Canto I, stanza 133).

13. Alvin B. Kernan, *The Plot of Satire* (New Haven: Yale University Press, 1965).

14. Mikhail Bakhtin, *Problems of Dostoevsky's Poetics*, tr. Caryl Emerson (Minneapolis: University of Minnesota Press, 1984), p. 111.

15. Albert O. Hirschman, *The Rhetoric of Reaction: Perversity, Futility, Jeopardy* (Cambridge, Mass.: Harvard University Press, 1991), p. 37.

16. John Stuart Mill, *Autobiography* (Indianapolis: Library of Liberal Arts, 1957), p. 44.

17. Perhaps it was the loss of satiric freedom in tendentious argument that Bakhtin had in mind when he noted the superiority of Dostoevsky's novels over his journalism, as in *Problems of Dostoevsky's Poetics*, pp. 91–92.

18. Marilyn Butler, *Jane Austen and the War of Ideas* (Oxford: Clarendon, 1975).

19. The Houyhnhnms have no laws; nor does the Party pass laws in *Nineteen Eighty-four*.

20. Walter J. Ong, S.J., "Swift on the Mind: The Myth of Asepsis," *Modern Language Quarterly* 15 (1954), 219. Ong's strictly hostile reading itself ignores the jokers in Swift's deck.

21. Jonathan Swift, *The Mechanical Operation of the Spirit*, in *A Tale of a Tub and Other Works* (Oxford: Oxford University Press, 1986), p. 129.

22. Richard Ellmann, *The Consciousness of Joyce* (Toronto: Oxford University Press, 1977), p. 89.

23. Alexander Herzen, *My Life and Thoughts*, tr. Constance Garnett (Berkeley: University of California Press, 1982), p. 417.

24. Isaiah Berlin, Introduction to Herzen, *My Life and Thoughts*, p. xix.

25. Hannah Arendt, *Totalitarianism* (Volume Three of *The Origins of Totalitarianism*) (New York: Harcourt, Brace and World, 1968), pp. 168–69.

26. In pointing out the exploitation of satire by political interests, I do not mean to assert a moral equivalence among them. Totalitarianism has no equivalent. I am interested in the nonequivalence of satire and its several political translations, which is to say the quality of freedom lost in passage.

27. Isaiah Berlin, *Four Essays on Liberty* (London: Oxford University Press, 1969).

28. Bakhtin, *Problems of Dostoevsky's Poetics*, p. 114.

29. Used by both Lenin and Stalin, the phrase is cited by Arendt, *Totalitarianism*, p. 170.

30. In *The Kreutzer Sonata*, dominated by a single authoritative voice of disgust, we witness satire hardening into a kind of creed. A more novelistic tale would leave us in greater doubt about the sanity of the protagonist, Pozdnyshev. In any case, the mind's habit of obscuring things—that is, our addiction to "false consciousness"—is brought out in this work with great intensity.

31. In liberal society, for its part, the medical metaphors used by Lady Philosophy as she treats her patient come to life in the figure of the therapist. The reports of our healers' deep probes into the mind prove no less hollow than the ideological formulas they profess to transcend. See Stewart Justman, *The Psychological Mystique* (Evanston: Northwestern University Press, 1998).

Index